THE ORIGINS OF THIGH STRE

89

9

The Origins of the Social Democratic Party

Noel Tracy

FLINDERS POLITICS MONOGRAPHS—No. 1

CROOM HELM
London & Canberra

© 1983 N. Tracy
Croom Helm Ltd, Provident House, Burrell Row,
Beckenham, Kent BR3 1AT

British Library Cataloguing in Publication Data

Tracy, Noel
    The origins of the Social Democratic Party.—
    (Flinders politics monographs; no. 1)
    1. Social Democratic Party—History
    I. Title   II. Series
    324.241'0972'09   JN1129.5/

    ISBN 0-7099-2426-7

Printed in Great Britain by
Biddles Ltd, Guildford, Surrey

TABLE OF CONTENTS

FLINDERS POLITICS MONOGRAPHS

A Series of Monographs in Politics and Related Disciplines

Series Editor: Dean Jaensch
Flinders University

The Flinders Politics Monographs consist of discrete studies of topics, themes and contemporary political issues which will be of interest to a wide audience in the Social Sciences.

The Series is edited in the Discipline of Politics, Flinders University, South Australia. Authors proposing a manuscript for inclusion in the Series should first send a brief abstract to:

The Editor,
Flinders Politics Monographs,
Discipline of Politics,
Flinders University,
Bedford Park,
South Australia, 5042.

INTRODUCTION

This essay was originally completed in September 1981. However, such are the vagaries of publishing at the current time, that it is unlikely to see the light of day before the second half of 1982. Despite the advantages of hindsight, I decided against any substantial rewriting and to let it stand for what is was; a first estimation. In justification of this course of action, I can only say that I consider the basic arguments remain sound and that I am and indeed was more concerned with underlying trends than blow for blow details. I have, however, added a postscript and updated a number of footnotes.

I became interested in the causes of the Social Democratic split from the British Labour Party during a visit to England at the end of 1980. Indeed, I was present in London during the fateful Special Conference of the Labour Party in January 1982 following immediately upon which the first formal steps in the split were made by "the gang of three" as David Owen, William Rodgers and Shirley Williams were then known.

At the time the press, radio and television were virtually unanimous that "the gang" were quitting after an unsuccessful battle to preserve the social democractic nature of the party in the face of an onslaught from the "extreme left". "The gang" were seen as the now isolated heirs of Hugh Gaitskell and Anthony Crosland finally forced to leave the party in which they had spent all their political lives as the battle was lost. The corollary of this was that the Labour Party was in the hands of the fundamentalist left. Both propositions struck me at the time, as being palpably false. "The gang" far from representing a continuation of the social democratic politics outlined by Anthong Crosland twenty-five years previously in The Future of Socialism represented a complete break with them. At the same time the actual policies, although not always the rhetoric, being put forwaard by Tony Benn and the left and adopted by the Party Conference, did not seem to me to have departed all that far from those previously outlined by Crosland. As a result I decided to investigate the causes of the split and the present essay is the result.

To some extent, this essay became an investigation into the fate of Keynesianism in the Labour Party. I was even tempted to insert "A Keynesian Critique" as a subtitle to the finished product. I rejected the idea as it would have given the impression that I was both a Keynesian and an economist by profession: neither of which was true. The essay however, is certainly written within a Keynesian paradigm. The reasons for doing so are fairly clear: the debates on economic policy within the party have all been concerned one way or another with the assumptions and remedies proposed by the Keynesian system while at the same time all the principle actors in this story have taken it as their point of reference.

My thanks are due to Andy Mack, Richard DeAngelis, Steve Reglar and Constance Lever for their encouragement and critical support throughout the preparation of this essay. Responsibility for errors, omissions and opinions, however, remain mine alone.

Noel Tracy,
Flinders University,
Adelaide.

FROM REFORMISM TO SOCIAL DEMOCRACY

The history of the recent split in the Labour Party is the history of the distintegration, in the face of economic reality, of the ideas on which the social democratic current in the party was based. This may seem a somewhat sweeping statement particularly in view of the fact that the split, when it finally came, was certainly over organisational questions, but to accept that is to take too simplistic a view and to fail to distinguish between underlying causes and proximate causes. The position of the "social democrats" was undermined long before the organisational changes introduced in the wake of the crushing 1979 electoral defeat.

"The party I loved and worked for over so many years no longer exists" wrote Shirley Williams in her letter of resignation from the National Executive Committee of the Labour Party in February this year (The Times, 10.2.81, p. 1). It is therefore pertinent to look at the nature of the Labour Party in which the leading members of the new Social Democratic Party came to play a leading role. An investigation of the political biographies of the leading members of the SDP - Roy Jenkins, David Owen, Shirley Williams and Bill Rodgers - reveals that, with the exception of Owen, who is somewhat younger than the others (42 at the time of writing), they came to prominence in the party in the 1950s. Jenkins entered parliament in 1948, after the initial reformist wave of the 1945 government was already spent. Williams unsuccessfully contested seats in 1954, 1955, and 1959, finally becoming an MP in 1964. Rodgers began by contesting a by-election in 1957 and was elected in another by-election in 1962. All three were leading supporters of Hugh Gaitskell in the Campaign for Democratic Socialism and in his fights with the left over public ownership and unilateral nuclear disarmament after the landslide general election defeat in 1959 - and all three held office in the Wilson government formed in 1964, although Williams was only a PPS (Who's Who 1980, p. 1336, pp. 2189-90, p. 2753; P. Williams 1979, pp. 537-653). In this, they are of a different generation from all those who have led the party in the post-war period: Atlee, Gaitskell, Wilson, Callaghan and now Foot, all of whom were men of '45. This generational gap is significant, for the 1950s were the years in which the Labour Party engaged in a significant debate as to whether it was a reformist socialist party or a social democratic party and moved programmatically towards the latter position. I am not at all trying to argue that Wilson and Callaghan were not social democrats in word and deed, but that unlike the "Gang of Four" they had roots in another period of the party's history as well. They were converts to social democracy and its Keynesian base, were less sure of its viability and were more committed to the party's traditional alliance with the trade unions.

Reformist Socialism and Social Democracy

How are we to distinguish clearly between reformist socialism, some-times called democratic socialism, and social democracy? I think it is fairly clear. Reformist socialism is committed to the transformation of society by the transfer of ownership of the instruments of economic power from private to public hands, however gradually it is to be attained.

Democratic socialism maintains that economic change is necessary for social change. Capitalism must be transformed into socialism by a series of institutional changes.

Social democracy on the other hand envisages a large measure of social reform within the existing parameters of society. The state will be interventionist but institutional change will be limited. It is essentially a difference over the importance of the question of ownership of the means of production. However a certain amount of historical enquiry will clarify the position.

Labour's pre-Keynesian Reformist Socialism

Under these definitions, the British Labour Party since its founding conference in 1918 has been a reformist socialist party in terms of its aims. All the intellectual currents that came together to form the British Labour Party - Fabianism, Marxism, Owenism and even Christian Socialism - assumed the need for fundamental change in the ownership of economic institutions. All assumed full public ownership to be necessary, although how the resulting structure was to be administered was a matter of some debate. Proposals ranged from Fabian bureaucratic centralism to Owenist co-operatives, the Christian Socialists "Socialist Commonwealth" and the Guild Socialists "workers control" (Crosland, 1956, pp. 81-86). The architect of Clause IV of the Party Constitution, which committed it to the nationalisation of the means of production, distribution and exchange, was the right-wing Fabian, Sydney Webb. Early Labour leaders like MacDonald and Snowden saw Labour's task as the gradual supercession of the capitalist system. At the founding conference, MacDonald outlined his programme:

> A parliamentary election will give us all the power
> that Lenin had to get by a revolution, and such a
> majority can proceed to effect the transition from
> capitalism to socialism with the co-operation of
> the people and not merely by edict (Cited by
> Coates, 1975, pp. 139-140).

This is not to say that the party always contested elections on a maximum programme. On the contrary, and this was essentially the problem, it tended to enter elections proposing no more than a few minimal ad hoc reforms and with an economic programme that was little different from other parties. The party, in common with other reformist socialist parties lacked any sort of intermediate programme for economic management which would have permitted it to deal with the economic difficulties it faced in government. There was a total vacuum between the maximum programme (socialism) and the practical reforms that could be introduced. In this respect in 1924, and 1929, Chancellor of the Exchequer Phillip Snowden with Macdonald's support saw his prime task as being to reduce the National Debt. In fact in 1924, at a time of very high unemployment, he used a budget surplus of 48 million pounds to repay part of this debt (Colin Cross cited by Coates, 1975, pp. 137-138), exactly the policy an orthodox fiscal conservative would have followed. The Labour Party was not alone in this; in Germany, the Marxist Rudolf Hilferding was adamant that an economic depression "had to run its course" (Bell, 1977, p. 91). The final indignity for the Labour Party came when MacDonald and Snowden led a minority of the 1929-31 Labour Government into alliance

2.

with the Conservatives on the issue of reducing unemployment pay with more than 3 million unemployed. The dilemma of having no economic programme for dealing with the day to day problems of the capitalist economy had come home to roost. (For a fuller discussion of reformist socialism's economic weaknesses see Przeworski, 1980; Strachey, 1952; Bell, 1977; Stokes and Slee, 1981).

The Keynesian Revolution

What changed the picture for socialist politicians was the Keynesian revolution in economic thought, for Keynes' demand-side economics gave them the means for a strong measure of influence in the capitalist economy without fundamental structural change on the supply side. In other words, it provided an immediate practical programme.

What Keynes did was to refute Say's Law and to suggest that its converse was nearer the reality. Jean-Baptiste Say (1767-1832) had maintained that every supply created its own demand and that therefore total supply must equal total demand. His theory was one of the foundation stones of the equilibrium theory of economics. This in turn maintained that long-term unemployment and excess capacity could not occur. They were a "hiccup" in the system which would soon right itself and return to equilibrium. The problem with Say's Law was that it was essentially based on a barter model and took too little account of money. Keynes argued that the equilibrium theory was false and that the mass unemployment of the interwar years, and especially after 1929, was caused by insufficient demand due to excess savings, excess insofar as they were greater than could be invested profitably domestically, themselves caused by the high rates of interest which the orthodox deflationary monetary programme required. A fallacy in the equilibrium theory of economics was the assumption that savings equalled investment. Keynes pointed out that many savers preferred money to tying up their savings in investment (liquidity preference) and that investment decisions were often made independently of the volume of savings as a result of business 'confidence'. This meant that in a depression, even if savings rose , investment would continue to fall due to the lack of profitable opportunities, while savings by reducing effective demand would deepen the depression. Keynes also realised that wages would not respond fully to a reduction of demand so that prices, which he saw as being determined by costs rather than supply and demand at least in the short term, would not fall in line with demand. A reduction in demand would therefore produce cuts in production and employment rather than falls in the levels of wages and prices. In effect, Keynes argued that if the government got demand right, problems on the supply side could be resolved. Keynes' short term programme was to reduce interest rates to encourage spending rather than savings, to pay the unemployed and to increase government employment; in general to increase demand enabling the private sector to return to full capacity working (Skidelsky, 1979, pp. 30-31; Reglar, 1982, p. 89).

Keynes' theories therefore provided socialist parties with an immediate programme for improving the conditions of their constituency. They could provide full employment, by far the most important political consideration for the working class, without major restructuring and intervention in the economy, by controlling effective demand, the means to do which was largely already in the hands of government. Increased reforms in the field of social welfare and education could also be justified even in hard times because they increased effective demand and therefore stimulated the private sector. However, while Keynes' insights provided socialist parties with short term policies, they tended to undermine their long term programme. If the economy could be regulated by control of demand, essentially a fiscal matter, was socialist planning and structural change any longer necessary? It is certainly true, as Stuart Holland and Steve Reglar amongst others have pointed out, that Keynes had considered the socialisation of investment and a degree of "moderate" planning a long term necessity and that this has been consistently overlooked by many self-professed Keynesians (Holland, 1978, pp. 21-22; Reglar, 1981). It is clear, however that Keynes never intended any system of socialist planning:

> ...a somewhat comprehensive socialisation of investment will prove the only means of securing an approximation to full employment...But beyond that no obvious case is made out for a system of State Socialism...It is not the ownership of the instruments of production which it is important for the State to assume...(Keynes, 1973, p. 378).

The achievement of Keynes for liberals was that he was able to reconcile management of the economy with a very large measure of economic free-will. He also suggested that the unemployment and depression of the inter-war years was less the result of class antagonisms than of the technical problem of oversavings, thus further undermining the socialist case. However, he did argue that a substantial redistribution in favour of lower income groups was necessary if demand was to be maintained and that his techniques could not be used merely to preserve the status quo.

There is a certain amount of evidence that the Labour Government of 1945-51 never fully reconciled themselves to the implications of the Keynesian revolution. Certainly most of their policies were Keynesian inspired but there were also measures of social transformation contained in the nationalisation programme. The electricity grid, the coal, steel, railways and road transport industries were nationalised as were docks and civil aviation. It was undoubtedly the case that coal and railways, certainly, and steel and docks, probably, were near bankrupt. However, it is less in the nationalisations themselves but in the assumptions held by many leading members that a programme of further nationalisations must go ahead, despite the problems of accountability and benefit that had become apparent, that the contradictions became clear. It was often those on the right wing of the party who were most insistent on the continuation of the programme, Herbert Morrison being the most important in this respect (Coates, 1975, p. 80). Morrison along with Bevin was the leader of the right wing and considered by many to be Atlee's heir-apparent. On leaving office in 1951, many Labour politicians showed that they had not fully absorbed Keynes' revolution. They expected a Tory government to result in mass unemployment in a short time (Coates, 1975, p. 80). Harold Wilson was fairly typical of this:

4.

Slump conditions are spreading slowly across the country aided by the financial policy of the government and we are facing dollar crisis and unemployment at the same time. The crisis when it finally comes will therefore not be a repetition of 1947 and 1949. It will be another 1931 (Wilson, The Times, 7.6.52 cited Foot, 1968 p. 112).

In case it should be thought this was an abberation, he was still predicting a 1931 type slump more than a year later (Labour Party Conference Report 1953, ibid, p. 112).

Keynesian Social Democracy

However, while there was confusion in some quarters, the full implications of Keynesianism had become clear in others. On his appointment as Chancellor in 1950, Hugh Gaitskell outlined what he saw as the role of future Labour Chancellors:

> ...over the next 10 years the principal task of a Socialist Chancellor would be the redistribution of wealth, which unlike the greater equalisation of incomes was not generally accepted; once that was accomplished, the philosophical differences between the parties would gradually diminish and their rivalry would turn increasingly - as in the United States - into a competition in governmental competence (cited Saville, 1980, p. 160).

But it is only with the work of Anthony Crosland that the full debate about the implications of Keynes for the Labour Party really began. Crosland was undoubtedly the Labour Party's most substantial post-war theorist and, his major work, The Future of Socialism published in 1956 (he had published a shorter essay in 1952 along the same lines), laid the basis both philosophically and programmatically for the social democrats' battle for the soul of the party. There had been previous attempts to do this, most notably by Evan Durbin in 1940, but these had not had the influence they perhaps deserved, almost certainly because the time was not apposite. In the mid-1950s, with the world economy on the up and the Tories pursuing policies not much different from Labour, it was.

Crosland's basic assumption, in line with many neo-Keynesians, was that Keynesian demand management had effectively resolved the problem of the trade cycle with its propensity to boom and slump and that therefore capitalism and the mixed economy were on a relatively easy road to sustained growth in the future (Crosland, 1956, p. 396). There is little evidence that Keynes himself had gone this far as his views on the necessity of the socialisation of investment and long term problem of profits indicated (Keynes, 1973, pp. 163-4; pp. 315-320). Crosland argued that the "business class" had lost so much power to the state, now responsible for over 50% of investment, which coupled with transfer of effective control of business to managers rather than owners and government fiscal controls, meant that the post-war mixed economy could no longer even be regarded as capitalist at all (ibid, pp. 26-27; p. 24; p. 76). As a result he regarded economic questions as now secondary:

> I no longer regard questions of growth and efficiency as being, on the long view of primary importance to socialism. We stand, in Britain, on the threshold of mass abundance; and within a decade the average family will enjoy a standard of living which whether or not it fully satisfied their aspirations will certainly convince the reformer that he should turn his main attention elsewhere (ibid, p. 515).

The reasons were fairly clear: he did not evisage major economic problems re-occuring:

> Traditionally or at least since Marx, socialist thought has been dominated by the economic problems posed by capitalism: poverty, mass unemployment, squalor, instability, and even the possibility of the imminent collapse of the whole system. These were problems of the most severe and urgent character, and it was correct to argue that major economic changes must precede the execution of socialist policy in other fields. But it is gradually ceasing to be correct today. Capitalism has been reformed almost out of recognition. Despite occasional minor recessions and balance of payments crises, full employment and at least a tolerable degree of stability are likely to be maintained. (ibid, 1956, p. 517).

Crosland, along with most neo-Keynesians had re-introduced the neo-classical concept of "natural equilibrium", which Keynes had refuted, into their version of Keynesian economics (Reglar, 1982).

As well as his attack on traditional pre-occupations with economics and economic transformation, Crosland also launched an attack on the centrality of nationalisation and public ownership to socialism. Crosland did not only argue, as he might have done, that with the underlying problems of the trade cycle resolved, nationalisation was no longer necessary, but rather that nationalisation could not resolve the problems of the working class at the point of production. Arguing against the Marxists he maintained that peasant society was the only one in which the direct producer was not separated from the means of production necessarily, and that following nationalisation the working class would remain alienated from the means of production and forced into confrontation with the controllers of capital:

> Thus irrespective of who 'owns' the means of production in the legal sense, both 'confrontation' and 'alienation' are inevitable; and someone other than the mass of workers must ultimately make production decisions. The basic factor is not ownership but large scale (ibid, 1956, pp. 69-70).

If nationalisation could not resolve the problems of the working class and if the government had sufficient power at its disposal from fiscal and

monetary policies and through state economic activity, the utility of maintaining the mixed economy in terms of consensus politics was obvious. And
furthermore, as most of the natural monopolies, basic raw materials, public
utilities and infrastructure, had already been nationalised, any future
nationalisation must be with a view to establishing competitive public
enterprises i.e. nationalising firms rather than industries and making them
compete with other private sector firms (ibid, pp. 480-482). Crosland
summed up his economic attitudes by turning a statement by Harold Laski
on its head. Laski had maintained that political power would in fact belong
to the owners of economic power whatever the form of the state. Crosland
now wrote:

> It would be more accurate to turn Laski's state-
> ment on its head: Whatever the modes of economic
> production, economic power will, in fact, belong to
> the owners of political power and these today are
> certainly not the pristine class of capitalists (ibid,
> p. 29).

In summary Crosland's economic thought was unbridled optimism
based upon the ability to resolve economic problems by technical means.

What then should the socialist programme look like? In Crosland's
view:

> We can only venture very general statements of the
> objective. I feel clear that we need large egali-
> tarian changes in our education system, the distri-
> bution of property, the distribution of resources in
> periods of need, social manners and style of life,
> and the location of power within industry; and
> perhaps some, but certainly a smaller change in
> respect of income from work. I think that these
> changes...will amount to a considerable social
> revolution. On the other hand, I am sure that a
> definite limit exists to the degree of equality which
> is desirable (ibid, pp. 216-217).

For Crosland, socialism and equality required the relative transfer of
resources from private consumption to public expenditure. Greater
equality was to be obtained by improving the 'social wage', the welfare
services and public capital to which all were entitled as of right, rather
than by income levelling. However, he did not underestimate the greater
importance of transfers as opposed to universal provision for the poor, and
the resolution of the problem of poverty (ibid, pp. 146-147).

Another important element of the new philosophy was that the
capitalist class could be relied upon to play the game and to accept the
change. This, allied to Labour's traditional confidence in the neutrality of
the state, under-pinned the optimistic picture:

> Pre-war socialists often anticipated violent, if not
> unconstitutional opposition from private business,
> and a whole theory of 'capitalist sabotage' ranging
> from a flight of capital abroad to a 'strike of
> capital' at home was constructed on this premise.
> The event was very different (ibid, p. 29).

This then was the atmosphere in which Jenkins, Williams and Rodgers came to prominence in the party. Labour fought the 1959 election essentially on the questions of the redress of social privilege and social reform and economic questions were clearly secondary (Coates, 1975, p. 100). The party was defeated by a landslide. However, instead of accepting that the evident prosperity of the period had favoured the incumbent government and accepting it as a fact of life in politics, Gaitskell and to a lesser extent Crosland blamed Labour's defeat on the party's continuing commitment to full public ownership (Crosland, 1960). Gaitskell was only saying what had been a reality for some time. If you are no longer committed to full public ownership, why continue to keep it in the Party Constitution when it was an electoral albatross? Gaitskell lost this battle because he could not convince the trade union leaders to accept it. Jenkins, Williams and Rodgers were among Gaitskell's leading supporters in this debate as they were on the question of unilateral nuclear disarmament, the other debate which threatened to split the party assunder in the post-election defeat depression. However, while Gaitskell lost the debate on the Party Constitution, he won the unilateralism vote after a narrow defeat, and the de facto direction of the party continued in the direction Gaitskell intended. The social democratic current was wholly in the ascendancy when Gaitskell, at the height of his power, suddenly died of a mysterious illness and a new era in the party's history began, soon to be followed by a period of government and a first serious challenge to many social democratic assumptions.

2.
THE FAILURE OF SOCIAL DEMOCRACY: THE WILSON GOVERNMENT 1964-1970

Despite the optimism with which Labour entered office in 1964, within 100 days it was in full retreat in the face of external constraints, most notably the speculative run on the pound engendered by the balance of payments problems which had appeared in the last months of the Conservative government and had accelerated with Labour's election. Admittedly, by the mid-1960s, both Crosland himself (Crosland, 1962; Crosland, 1965) but more particularly the new Labour Leader Wilson had begun to realise that the optimism of Crosland's original "revisionist" thesis regarding economic growth had been somewhat misplaced. The whole emphasis of Labour's 1964 electoral manifesto had switched from social reform to improving Britain's economic performance. It was not that the former had been abandoned, far from it, but there was explicit acceptance that the former depended upon the latter. Wilson himself even went so far as to admit "there is no solution to our problems except on the basis of expanding output, expanding investment and rising productivity" (cited by Coates, 1975, p. 99) and, while the earlier Crosland would not have disagreed, the change was that it was now considered problematic. Nothing typified Labour's mood more than Wilson's 'white heat of technology' speech:

> We are restating our socialism in terms of the
> scientific revolution...The Britain that is going to
> be forged in the white heat of this revolution will
> be no place for...out-dated methods on either side
> of industry (ibid, p. 99).

However, there was one subtle change in Labour's commitment to social reform. The 1964 Manifesto read:

> The key fact in determining the speed at which new
> and better levels of benefit can be introduced will
> be the rate at which the British Economy can
> expand.

Previously, the assumption of Labour's programmes had been that redistribution would make a substantial contribution to the cost of social reforms. There was a growing awareness of economic restraints on social reform (Kincaid, 1971, p. 73) which predated the problems which would blow Labour's whole programme off course within months.

Sterling Crisis Produces a Non-Keynesian Response

On entering office in October 1964, Labour found an $800m deficit on the balance of payments. This deficit was the combined effect of trade imbalance and capital movements (Times, 27.10.64, p. 10). The attack on the pound was essentially speculative, however, and showed itself to be so conclusively when it continued even after substantial improvements occurred in the balance of trade. If the sterling crisis was in response to trading difficulties and therefore requiring a parity adjustment, it should

9.

have ended once the trading deficit was reversed. Even the October figures published a month after Labour took office showed exports up and imports down (Times, 18.11.64, p. 12) and this pattern continued throughout 1965 and 1966. The current account figures show this clearly:

Table 1: Balance of Payments on Current Account, 1964-66
(million pounds)

1964	- 376
1965	- 52
1966	+ 83

(Source: M. Artis in Beckerman, 1972, p. 298)

Despite the improvement, speculative attacks on the parity of sterling continued with monotonous regularity.

Labour's response was somewhat mixed (Times, 26.11.64, p. 12). The first reaction was to impose a 15% surcharge on manufactured imports (Times, 29.10.64, p. 12), a direct attack on the problem in the Keynesian manner. However, the blasts of protest this produced from Britain's trading partners in EFTA soon forced Wilson to retreat and accept that it could only be a temporary measure. Wilson, however, did refuse the demands of Lord Cromer, the Governor of the Bank of England for a wage freeze, cuts in government expenditure and a credit squeeze in November 1964 (Times, 26.11.64, p. 12) but he raised bank rate by 2% to a record peacetime 7%, increased taxes and borrowed $3000m from the IMF (Times, 24.11.64, p. 12; 26.11.64, p. 12). Callaghan's budget in the Spring of 1965 was deflationary and was accompanied by further IMF drawings (Times, 5.5.65 p. 17; 11.5.65, p. 12). Further speculative attacks in July led to cuts in government expenditure (Times, 28.7.65, p. 10) and finally in July 1966 Labour introduced massive expenditure cuts, further deflationary measures and a legally binding wage freeze (Foot, 1968, p. 181). The National Plan, introduced early in 1965 with much fanfare, was officially abandoned and with it any real prospects of rapid economic growth. The National Plan itself was merely indicative, being mostly concerned with swapping information and publishing industry's own targets (A. Graham in Beckerman, 1972, p. 182; Howell, 1976, p. 283), and was not as important in itself as was the psychological blow its abandonment dealt to Labour's hopes. The "pristine class of capitalists", or at least one section of them, the international financiers, who in Crosland's view had lost so much power to the state in the post-war period, had proved themselves more than able to blow a government off course particularly in the international context which he had scarcely discussed. Another major factor in the 1964 run on sterling had been the 650-700 million pounds transferred out of sterling by multi-national companies operating in Britain of which only 100 million pounds could be accounted for by growth of trade (Peter Shore cited Coates, 1975, p. 110).

The pattern set in the early years of the first Wilson government continued until it lost office in 1970. It has often been argued that the small majority Labour had in 1964 imposed constraints, but the large majority gained in 1966 did not seem to change its behaviour a great deal. Even when Labour finally devalued the pound in 1967, the deflationary policies continued, putting a firm damper on any prospects of domestic recovery. When it lost office, while the balance of payments were in healthy surplus, unemployment and inflation were substantially up and economic growth and investment substantially down on what they had been when Labour took office (A. Graham in Beckerman, 1972, p. 206; M. Artis, ibid, p. 298).

It was not that Labour's preoccupation with social reform led to their entering office in 1964 unprepared for the economic problems they faced as some have suggested (Coates, 1975, p. 107). The balance of payments constraint was not new and Labour's response had been discussed at great length in opposition. Labour's response to balance of payments problems was to be Keynesian and not monetarist as the following indicates:

> (The Labour Government) should be prepared to go through a period of weak balance of payments...a period of losing reserves if necessary, in order to get over the hump of stepping up our rate of growth (Roy Jenkins to 1961 Conference, : Coates, 1975, p. 102).

> ...which do the Government want most? Do they want stagnation here and firm balance of payments, or do they want growth and to handle the difficulties that would arise in the balance of payments as they occur? I would choose the second (James Callaghan to 1961 Conference, ibid, p. 102).

> For twelve years, the Conservative Government has relied on the outdated technique of monetary regulation of the economy. This necessitated excessive interest rates and led to insufficient investment and innovation (Harold Wilson, 1964, p. 17).

Keynesian Tools Prove Too Controversial

It was not only that the international financiers could thwart a government's programme but also that the Keynesian tools for remedying the situation were not implemented. The Keynesian response to a trade imbalance was fairly clear: devaluation or import restrictions or possibly a rush for growth. In 1931, Keynes clearly favoured devaluation but by 1933 he had moved towards a preference for tariff protection. Neo-Keynesianism on the other hand continued to favour devaluation (Keynes, 1931, p. 285; Keynes, 1933; Crosland, 1965, pp. 13-14). The blast of protest from Britain's trading partners and the threats of retaliation at the introduction of a 15% tariff surcharge showed the limits to the direct controls that could be implemented. Devaluation was clearly the simplest option but it had serious problems. It could produce retaliatory devaluations and by increasing the cost of imports could be inflationary. The United States also feared that a British devaluation would lead to a speculative attack on the dollar which could possibly bring down the whole international monetary system. And it meant confrontation with the City of London, whose leading members were demanding orthodox deflationary measures and whose power to sabotage government was now apparent as their part in the sterling crisis had shown.

The problem was that the Keynesian remedies were not consensus politics; rather they meant confrontation with the financial barons of the City or a trade war with Britain's competitors. Wilson also opposed devaluation because he felt it would lead to featherbedding in industry and inflation (Wilson, 1964, p. 33; Foot, 1968, p. 181-182). In the sterling crisis of 1966, Jenkins, Brown and Crosland urged devaluation since the alternatives had now become massive deflation, but Wilson carried the day (Foot, 1968, pp. 181-182; Stewart, 1974, p. 24).

The Balance Sheet of 6 Years of Deflation

The net result of six years of deflation was that Labour failed to achieve the economic targets it had set itself in 1964. The National Plan had aimed at a growth rate of 4 per cent but only 1.7% was achieved (Bacon and Eltis, 1975, p. 11). In retrospect, Crosland blamed the slow growth on the "stop go" policies of successive governments and the slow growth of productivity. (Crosland, 1975, p. 81). There is no doubt that he was correct in the case of the former but a considerable question mark has to be raised against the latter.

During the years of the Labour Government, productivity in industry rose faster than it had done during the previous ten years and almost exactly in line with the National Plan projections. Productivity grew by 4% p.a. 1964-1970 against only 3% p.a. in the previous decade. The difference was that in the previous decade production rose in line with productivity gains whereas in the latter period, productivity gains were used for a series of defensive rationalisations whose aim was less to increase production than to produce the same amount more efficiently. The end result of this was rising unemployment and a declining industrial base (Bacon and Eltis, 1975, p. 35-36; A. Graham, in Beckerman, 1972, p. 200). By 1970 the declining competitiveness of British industry (Blackburn, 1971, p. 6; Britain's share of world trade had fallen from 16.5% in 1960 to 10.% in 1970 despite a 15% devaluation), combined with six years of severe deflation, had begun to take its toll on British industry. Profits were down considerably as was company liquidity as the following tables show:

Table 2: Company Profits as % of Capital Investment, 1959-69

	1955/9	60/64	64	65	66	67	68	69
Pre-tax	17.3	14.7	14.9	14.3	11.9	12.3	12.6	10.9
Post-tax	8.4	7.3	7.1	7.9	5.8	6.0	4.8	3.2

(Source: A. Graham in Beckerman, 1972, p. 207).

Company Liquidity	Undistributed Profits as % of capital investment	Bank Loans as % of capital investment
1965	114.8	20.3
1966	105.3	7.6
1967	107.0	13.9
1968	109.4	21.6
1969	87.4	21.9
1970	63.5	33.3

(Source: Times, 16.6.75 cited by Field, 1979, p. 99).

Britain was also the only OECD Country in which industrial employment declined absolutely before 1973. In other countries, most notably the USA and Sweden, it declined relative to total employment but the number of jobs in industry increased (L. Lenkowski, in Tyrell Jnr., 1977, pp. 159-160). The decline of profits did not mean, as sections of the press were claiming, that wages were gaining as a result. Certainly money wages were up but the growth of net real income of manual workers during the period of the Labour government rose by little more than half a percent per year, less than half of what they had risen in the last five years of the Conservative Government and a mere quarter of the rise in the five years before that (Crosland, 1975, p. 25).

The decline of profitability and competitiveness of British industry was also despite growing state subsidies during the period. Between 1964 and 1974, direct aid to industry rose from 4% to 7% of GNP of which the giant companies were the major beneficiaries. Michael Barratt-Brown estimates that by 1970, state aid to industry was equivalent to half of all private sector fixed capital formation excluding dwellings (Barratt-Brown, 1971, p. 199; Hatfield, 1979, p. 36).

Defeat and Disillusion

By 1970, the serious structural problems of British industry, antiquated capital stock, declining competitiveness vis-a-vis the rising industrial stars (West Germany, Japan and France), severe industrial relations problems resulting from strong unions, both nationally and at shop floor level, in conditions of low growth adopting defensive attitudes towards new techniques, and the tendency to suck in imports as soon as government restraints on demand were relaxed, were clearly visible. The Labour years had seen all these problems accentuate and none of them seemed reversible by the Keynesian techniques at the disposal of government without confrontation from which the government had shied away and Labour fell from office in 1970 in a mood of demoralisation.

Looking back on Labour's defeat in 1970, a somewhat rueful Crosland admitted:

> ...I was too complacent about growth...I accepted
> the official projections which forecast a nearly
> stationary population; hence...I did not foresee the
> large demands on our resources...which a rising
> population brings in its train. And I did not anti-
> cipate that successive governments would be so
> eccentric as to use periodic bouts of deflation...as
> almost their only means of regulating the economy
> (Crosland, 1975(a), p. 73).

However, he did not anticipate that Labour now needed some great
shift of direction but rather a clear affirmation of agreed ideas particularly
on equality (ibid, pp. 72-73). In future, he recognised that Labour must
alter its priorities in favour of economic growth, the most important means
to which he saw as a greater flexibility of exchange rates (ibid, pp. 81-82).
But, in reality, this had been Labour's attitude before 1964 which had been
quickly abandoned in office.

Crosland was also concerned with the serious effect Labour's
economic failure had had on the social programme. Crosland had always
identified socialism with equality and equality with public provision:

> Socialism and equality require a relative transfer
> of resources from private consumption to public
> expenditure...but under conditions of slow growth,
> efforts to achieve these transfers inevitably pro-
> voke inflation. For since they cannot come from
> the fruits of rapid growth, they must come from
> higher taxation of existing incomes. But higher
> indirect taxes put up prices; higher direct taxes
> provoke compensating claims for higher money,
> wages and salaries. In our slow growth economy
> the shift away from personal consumption has
> harshly exacerbated the problem of inflation (ibid,
> p. 26).

For the future, any transfer of resources from private to public
consumption, which was not of itself inflationary, could only come about "if
the absolute level of consumption is rising steadily; and that requires a
rapid rate of growth" (ibid, p. 57). At times he was even more pessimistic.
Re-allocation of resources was not only difficult because of the
inflationary pressures engendered, but impossible in a democracy in the
absence of growth:

> I do assert dogmatically that in a democracy low or
> zero growth wholly excludes the possibility. In a
> utopia (or a dictatorship) perhaps we might transfer
> x percent of a near static GNP towards 8 million
> pensioners, better housing and cleaning up
> pollution; in a rough democratic world in which we
> live, we cannot (ibid, p. 76).

Under the Labour Government public spending had climbed from 41%
of GNP in 1964 to 49% by 1970 (Crosland, 1975(a), p. 33). It should be
noted however that this includes transfers which are really part of private

spending; nonetheless, net government spending probably rose from 25% to nearly 30% of GNP in the Labour years (Gough, 1979, pp. 81-84). The net effect of increasing public expenditure in conditions of slow growth and inflation was that the burden of taxation, particularly on the lower paid, increased. In 1950, a manual worker on average wages paid no income tax at all, by 1960 his tax and national insurance contributions had risen to 8% of his earnings, but by 1970 they took almost 20%. The major reason was that the government did not index tax allowances, thereby allowing inflation to bring more and more people into the tax net. Between 1963/64 and 1969/70, the tax threshold of the average family (2 adults, 2 children) fell from 84.5% of average earnings to 56.1%. For a family with four children it was even worse, falling from 125.8% of average earnings to 75.6% (Field, 1977, p. 32). For the first time direct tax became a major cause of poverty in the working class (Coates, 1975, p. 114) and the now well-known poverty trap became established wherein a lower paid worker is better off on unemployment or sickness benefits or on social security handouts than he would be in work because of the tax situation; benefits are tax-free while wages are not. At about this time, James Kincaid was concluding that the incidence of tax throughout the community was about the same for all groups, except that the very poor paid proportionally more tax than average, and the highest income groups paid rather less than average (Kincaid, 1971, p. 41). Michael Barratt-Brown's investigations also concluded that the working class and even the poor paid for their own social services. In terms of transfers, he concluded only the lowest 10% of families were net beneficiaries. Nevertheless, the insurance aspect of the welfare state, however difficult to quantify, was undoubtedly beneficial to the lower social groups (Barratt-Brown, 1971, p. 196).

Crosland himself recognised that much of the increased spending on the social services under Labour had gone into creating large middle class bureaucracies rather than improving services (Crosland, 1975(b), p. 8), a conclusion that is amply illustrated by what was happening in the hospital and education services. Between 1964 and 1973 in the hospital service, there was a 51% increase in administrators and an 11% fall in beds; in education, employment grew by 54% but only half of it was concerned with teaching in the widest sense (W. Eltis, in Beckerman, 1978, pp. 124-126). Thus by the early 1970s a distinct question mark was being raised as to whether increased public spending was redistributing in favour of wage and salary earners or against them.

Another of Crosland's assumptions that had come unstuck by this time was the idea of a fundamental and irreversible shift in the percentage of total income now going to wage and salary earners. Crosland had laid great stress on this in his earlier work as evidence of the declining power of the wealthy. Crosland's assumptions were based on the work of Dudley Seers who had compared 1949 with 1938 and found that there had been a large increase in wages as a percentage of GNP and a sharp fall in rents, dividends and interest (Crosland, 1956, p. 49). However, it was now clear that what Seers had found was a "once-off" redistribution resulting from the war which had since been whittled away. Certainly, the larger cake meant that there was more to be distributed but the shares were now drifting back towards pre-war levels to the benefit of the middle classes rather than the very rich:

Table 3: Post-tax Income (pre-tax in brackets) by families, 1938-72 (percentages of total income including state benefits)

	1938	1949	1954	1964	1972
Top 10%	(38) 33	(33) 27	(30)	(29)	(27) 24
Next 20%	(21) 23	(25) 14	(27)	(28)	(31) 28
Lower 70%	(41) 44	(42) 59	(43)	(43)	(42) 48

(Post-tax figures for 1954 and 1964 are not available:
Source: Royal Commission of Incomes and Wealth, 1975, cited by Scase, 1975, pp. 55-58).

Clearly, by 1970 the social democrats in the Labour Party were in serious trouble. There could be no doubts as to the external constraints on the Government's freedom of manoeuvre in the shape of the international financial community, the problems of the sterling area and the growing clouds over the whole international monetary system itself. British industry's declining competitiveness was going to make balance of payments problems a constant worry for years to come. Inflation now cast a shadow over any prospects of rapid growth at home by means of increasing demand in a neo-Keynesian manner, even if British industry had been in the mood to do so, and increasing demand itself might well just suck in imports and create a new balance of payment crisis. And above all this was the question of how to modernise British industry and cut import dependence.

In addition to the economic problems, there was also the question of the social reform programme. A question mark had certainly been raised as to its efficacy in securing greater equality and was it, in the British context of stagnation, a major cause of inflation? It was not to say that the reforms of Labour years were all to be written off. The benefits improved and liberal legislation enacted were of value in themselves. But the question was were they a factor in securing greater equality and a redistribution in favour of the working class and the poor, or were they improving public access to welfare services at the expense of the latter's private consumption?

It was increasingly beginning to look as if perhaps "the high fliers" of the 1950s and early 1960s, like the Emperor, "had no clothes". The economic question was clearly not resolved and, if it were not, then many of their assumptions were inoperative as Crosland had by then recognised.

3.
SOCIAL DEMOCRACY RESTATED: THE RISE OF THE NEW LEFT IN OPPOSITION

After the election defeat in June 1970, Crosland blamed the failure to attain a reasonable rate of economic growth for Labour's defeat and the "eccentric" policy of using deflation as the only means of regulating the economy for the failure to attain a reasonable level of economic growth (Crosland, 1975(a), p. 73). However personally disappointed he was with Labour's performance, he did not see any reason for a change of direction in party thinking nor did he envisage that there would be any great demand for any such change:

> There is no analogy with the 1950s, when society had been changed out of recognition since the 1930s by full employment and the Welfare State, and where a fundamental rethinking was required. That is not the position today, and the evidence is the lack of any furious ideological ferment within the party. Of course, we must continuously adapt our detailed policies, and of course new problems will call for new policies, but the basic objectives remain wholly relevant and contemporary. What we need is not some great shift of direction, but a clear reaffirmation of these agreed ideals. These ideals all fundamentally relate to how we redistribute our wealth and allocate our resources; that is what socialism is about, and what divides the left from the right. We shall not get the allocation we want without a certain view of taxation and public expenditure, and of social control and responsibility. And we shall not get that without a healthy rate of economic growth (Crosland, 1975(a), pp. 72-73).

While he did not envisage any substantial changes in Labour's policies, a degree of pessimism as to the possibility of the transfer of resources on which the social democratic, and socialist for that matter, programme depended was beginning to emerge. He was now of the opinion that the democratic system itself would prevent any such redistribution in a country with an economy like Britain's:

> ...I do assert dogmatically that in a democracy low or zero growth wholly excludes the possibility. For any substantial transfer then involves not merely a relative but an absolute decline in the real incomes of the better-off half of the population...; and this they will frustrate (ibid, p. 74).

However, Crossland could not have been more wrong about the mood of the party, for the next two years would see a debate as wide ranging and fundamental as the debates of the 1950s of which he had been a prime mover.

On the surface there was ample evidence to support Crosland's view of the lack of ideological ferment. There was a high degree of demoralisation in the party and many of the more militant had quit for the extra-parliamentary left, then probably enjoying its highest level of post-war support. The party organisation reported that in 135 marginal constituencies, the local organisation had been substantially reduced by disenchantment with the Labour Government (Economist, 5.9.70, p. 21). At the 1970 Conference, both Barbara Castle, who had spearheaded the prices and incomes policy and attempts to curb the strike activity of trade unions, and Denis Healey, who as Minister of Defence had supported the US build up in Vietnam, were elected to the NEC by constituency members, reflecting the fact that the party membership had moved to the right in government. The demoralisation was best summed up by the decline in the party's popular vote which was now absolutely lower than in 1951 in a larger electorate. As Heath's majority was fairly small, this reflected a growing tendency to abstention, demonstrated in the following table:

Table 4: Labour Vote 1951-1970

	Electorate	Labour Vote	% of Electorate
1951	34.6m	13.9m	40.2
1970	39.3	12.2	31.0

(Source: Coates, 1975, p. 226).

To some extent the debate which followed in the years of opposition was prefigured by the Department of Economic Affairs in 1969. In a pamphlet, The Task Ahead, it had been admitted that one of the greatest problems facing the Department was that "what happened in industry was not under the control of government" (cited Holland, 1975, p. 25). There was also a growing body of opinion, although still a minority, which did not see Britain's economic problem as being a technical one caused by stop-go policies and the overuse of deflation to regulate the economy in a situation of balance of payments problems but rather a structural one caused by declining industries and regions and the need to modernise to increase competitiveness and cut import dependence (Johnson, 1968, pp. 71-73; Blackburn, 1971, pp. 6-8; Davenport, 1964). The debate itself got going and increased in intensity almost accidentally. After the election defeat, Wilson withdrew to write his memoirs and did not again take up his leadership responsibilities until 1972 (Hatfield, 1978, p. 24). At the same time the Chairmanship of the Party fell to the left in successive years and the chairmen were able to exercise a considerable influence in encouraging debate. Labour Party chairmen are not elected; the job passes around the National Executive Committe by rote, "buggin's turn". In 1970-71, it fell to Ian Mikardo, a member of the old left and in the following year to Tony Benn, who would, as a result of the debate, become the leader of the 'new' left. Benn had not previously been associated with the left. In many ways, he had been the prototype of Wilson's technocratic politician advancing the vision of the "white heat of technology" transforming Britain. The man, however, who came to play the role that Crosland had played in the 1950s was Stuart Holland, an ex-member of Wilson's political

18.

staff, who had not previously played any leading role in party affairs (ibid, p. 46; M. Meacher MP, 1981, p. 6).

A New Analysis

It is often assumed that what happened after 1970 was that, following the failure of the social democratic programme in the face of economic constraints, the party, or at least the left of it, swung back to the traditional socialist programme of large scale nationalisation. This however is a misreading of what happened. Neither Benn, who emerged as the political leader of the "new" left, nor Holland, its leading ideologist, was associated with the old left. In almost every way the alternative economic strategy that emerged was an extension of the revisionist analysis advanced by Crosland in the 1950s.

The discussion began when Mikardo persuaded the NEC to upgrade its policy sub-committees from advisory status to policy formulating status. It was not intended that they should decide policy but that the NEC would have to vote on their proposals and not just shelve them as they could do if the advisory status continued. The NEC accepted the change largely to persuade leading party figures and outside experts to participate again. In the latter years of the Wilson government, the sub-committees had virtually collapsed as their advice had been continually ignored (Hatfield, 1978, p. 41-42). A number of large sub-committees were subsequently established, the most influential of which was to be the industry sub-committee. The first proposals of this committee under Mikardo's chairmanship were very traditional. It proposed the setting up of a series of new public sector monopolies for the drug industry, the aircraft industry, computers, insurance and motors (ibid, pp. 52-53). Holland did not join the committee until 1971 when he was introduced by Bill Rodgers, who had been using him as an advisor on the House of Commons Expenditure committee. Holland was very much associated with the social democratic wing of the party and was a frequent contributor at the Conferences of the social democratic journal, Socialist Commentary (ibid, p. 46). With the arrival of Holland, the thinking of the Industry Committee experienced a new turn. Holland's major work The Socialist Challenge, completed in January 1974, was written while he was participating in the debates in the Industry Committee (Holland, 1975, p. 10).

Holland's argument, which centered on the growing tendency towards monopoly in the industrial sector and the dominance of multi-national companies in both the domestic economy and in world trade, was that the question of ownership of the means of production must return to the centre of socialist thought because this monopoly and dominance was undermining both government's ability to manage the domestic economy by demand management and the relative autonomy of the state itself. He argued that the contemporary crisis, which by then had added Mr. Heath's "boom and bust" and runaway inflation to the stagnation induced by Labour's six years of deflation, had not arisen from the misapplication of neo-Keynesian techniques of demand management, although he criticised Labour's 1964-67 policy as non-Keynesian (ibid, p. 19) but rather from their erosion by a new mode of production which had divorced macro-policy from micro-structure (ibid, p. 15). He pointed out how Mr. Heath's expansion of demand had not increased investment supply but had merely led to increased inflation (ibid, p. 15). Investment decisions were now being made on an international rather than a national basis and could by-pass unfavourable conditions in any particular country by such devices as transfer pricing and international movements of capital. Deflation could not counter inflation effectively because the large companies could raise prices unchecked by market constraints and could avoid a credit squeeze by their own capital transfers which also added to demand (money supply) at the same time (ibid, p. 80). Holland also suggested that international trade was no longer essentially between different companies in different countries but increasingly between the same companies in different countries (ibid, p. 75) which meant that price no longer controlled export volumes and was why Britain's devaluation, the American inflation and the West German revaluation, all of which should have assisted British exports, had not led to any long term improvement in the balance of payments (ibid, p. 76).

As a final proof of his contentions, Holland pointed to the strength of British-based companies. Of the top 500 companies in Europe, 140 were British, more even than were West German, while Britain's economic performance was worse than any of her European competitors. Britain still controlled a greater share of world multi-national investment than any other country, save the United States, and not much less than the rest of Europe and Japan combined (USA 48%, UK 20%, rest of Europe and Japan 25%). Furthermore, that more than 80% of this overseas investment by British companies was by 165 firms (ibid, p. 78). It was clear, he concluded, that these large multi-nationals were transferring their production overseas as they no longer saw Britain as a viable proposition for large scale investment.

A New Strategy

Holland's answer to the new problem was far from traditional: the state had to establish itself in the manufacturing sector and compete head on with the multi-nationals. He noted that Britain did not really have a mixed economy. The state was restricted to basic industries, services and infrastructure while the private sector had a free run in manufacturing. Thus there could not be state sector led growth because expansion in the state sector would not automatically lead to expansion in the private sector; more likely it would lead to unused capacity and it could have little or no impact on the export/import balance (ibid, pp. 146-147). The necessity was therefore to expand the state sector into manufacturing to produce a genuinely mixed economy, while permitting a very large measure of market criteria to continue to apply. It was futile to try to re-establish the lost liberal capitalist order; rather the state must now mobilise its own economic powers to ensure it served social and economic objectives ibid, pp. 164-169; pp. 177-178). He argued that there was a case for nationalising 25 of the top 100 manufacturing companies and turning them into new public enterprise leaders but, far from establishing new public sector monopolies, they must directly compete with remaining private sector firms in each sector if the full benefits were to be obtained:

> ...direct investment in new public enterprise can only harness the meso-economic power of the remaining private sector firms if it is represented in the main industrial sectors in which they operate. In other words (they) can only exert a pull effect on the other big firms if (they) are competing with them in the first place (ibid, pp. 184-185).

Holland's proposals for nationalising about 25 top manufacturing companies were very much related to two other ideas. The first was to establish a large State Holding Company (SHC) to co-ordinate the whole state sector, including the new state public enterprises. The model for this State Holding Company, as the NEC Public Sector Group admitted, was to be the Italian IRI (Hatfield, 1978, p. 145; Holland, 1975, p. 153; <u>Politics and Power 2</u>, pp. 16-17). The second was that companies with a turnover of over 50 million pounds per annum should be "invited" to enter into planning agreements with the state in respect of their investment programmes and export plans. The plans were to be drawn up by the companies themselves with the state holding reserve powers for use when the public interest was at risk. Holland envisaged state aid and allowances being withheld as sanction for non-compliance. It was envisaged that some 100 companies would be subject to Planning Agreements (Benn, 1979, p. 56). Again the models were European. Similar planning agreements were then in operation in France, Italy and Belgium (Holland, 1975, pp. 231-235). The plans for a SHC were also closely paralleled with similar developments in Europe. In Sweden a single SHC, the "Statsforetag" had been introduced in January 1970; in France, the Industrial Development Institute had been unveiled in March 1970 to promote new state activities; while in West Germany, the "Moller" proposals before the SPD government foresaw a new "super-holding". Similar proposals were being introduced in Belgium (Hatfield, 1978, p. 84). Holland clearly recognised that his proposals were essentially an extension of "state capitalism" but argued to reject such techniques was "to allow the devil some of the best tunes" and that such changes could be used for a wider social transformation (Holland, 1975, p. 154).

Contradictory Reactions

Initially, the social democrats supported the idea of a state holding company and the extension of the state's economic role into manufacturing (Hatfield, 1978, pp. 86-87). In a major speech in May 1972 to the National Union of Mineworkers, Roy Jenkins argued that neo-Keynesian techniques for managing the whole economy could no longer solve detailed problems, even when the problem was a whole region rather than a single firm. General demand management needed to be supplemented by more rigorous policies of direct intervention than those which Labour used between 1964 and 1970. He pointed approvingly to the fact that the Italian IRI and ENI controlled 370 firms and had played a major role in reversing the regional imbalance by siting new investments in the South. He stressed that to be effective the SHC had to represent a broad spectrum of industry (ibid, pp. 109-110). The response of the "old left" however was unsympathetic. A <u>Morning Star</u> editorial commented that "this programme is not for socialism but for the continuation of capitalism", while Eric Heffer, a leading left MP, added "the weakness of this approach to the subject of public ownership is that it begins to take the right road, but draws back at the decisive moment" (<u>ibid</u>, p. 130).

By early 1973, however, the social democrats were on the defensive and vigorously opposing both the scope of the SHC and the plans to nationalise large industrial companies. The reasons for the defensiveness of the social democrats, while never explicit, were almost certainly two-fold. First, they feared the growing strength of the "new left" grouped around a left social democratic programme in a way which they had never feared the "old left" because of its programmatic barrenness. Second, the social democrats were becoming isolated in the party both locally and in Parliament over the question of membership of the EEC, which they strongly supported and which the Party was opposed to on the terms negotiated by Heath. This rift and its seriousness became clear in October 1971. When Heath presented his terms for entering the EEC to Parliament. 69 Labour MPs led by the Deputy Leader Roy Jenkins and including most social democrats but not Crosland, voted with the Heath Government to accept the terms. A further 20 MPs abstained. This was despite a Party Conference decision only weeks earlier to reject Heath's terms. The Conference resolution had been carried by a majority of more than five to one. As 39 Tory MPs voted against, the votes of the 69 Labour members saved the Heath Government from defeat and a new general election (Stewart, 1974, pp. 111-112). Despite his behaviour, Jenkins was re-elected Deputy Leader a month later only to resign it the following January and leave the shadow cabinet when the NEC voted and Wilson accepted a resolution for a referendum on Britain's membership of the EEC when Labour returned to office (ibid, pp. 112-113). As a result, The Times began to speculate for the first time on the possibility of a split led by Jenkins and involving more than 20 Labour MPs (Times, 5.10.71, p. 1).

The rift widened when Dick Taverne MP, a social democrat, resigned from Parliament over the question of the EEC, forcing a by-election which he won as an Independent against an official Labour candidate in March 1973 (Stewart, 1974, p. 19).

When the social democrats launched their counterattack on the NEC, Crosland challenged Holland on the political and philosophical basis for his proposals. Holland turned the tables by naming Crosland's The Future of Socialism as a major influence. And in this he was undoubtedly correct for the forms of nationalisation now being proposed, i.e. competitive public enterprises, were what Crosland had recommended as a dynamic alternative to the public sector monopolies favoured by the party previously (Crosland, 1957, pp. 487-490; p. 492) and although they had not materialised had been part of the largely social democratic inspired programme in 1964 (Hatfield, 1978, p. 35).

The social democrats were on shaky ground, for while Holland's proposals, now adopted by the NEC, were more extensive and wide-ranging than they would have liked, there was no fundamental difference between them and policies they themselves had been recommending for years as a social democratic alternative to "old fashioned" "nationalise-everything" demands from the left. The Jenkins group among the social democrats seem to have recoiled from the idea of competitive public enterprise once they realised the implications. This, however, was not the case with the smaller group around Crosland. When the shadow cabinet discussed the proposals, now named "The Alternative Economic Strategy" (AES), the strongest critics were Harold Lever, Crosland and Shirley Williams, who attempted to defend the indefensible after the failure of 1964-70. They argued quite wrongly that the proposals were a crude drawback to the thinking of the 1930s and that a more sophisticated approach was needed in the light of modern economic management techniques and fiscal instruments of control, i.e. to rely on neo-Keynesian demand management and the increasingly discussed monetary controls by then enjoying a new intellectual vogue (Hatfield, 1978, p. 193). Only a year before, their leader, Roy Jenkin, and many of the other leading social democrats had been arguing how inadequate these techniques had been and would be in the future.

However, the Labour leader, Wilson, came to their rescue. Wilson had not spoken nor voted at the NEC meeting which adopted "A New Economic Strategy" but the next day he called a press conference to denounce the proposals, particularly the proposal to nationalise 25 top companies, making it clear that the shadow cabinet had a veto over the party's manifesto (ibid, p. 199). The social democrats also started to argue that the proposed SHC, now rechristened the National Enterprise Board (NEB), would be so big as to overbalance the relationship between itself and the democratically elected government. The National Enterprise Board must be rejected on democratic grounds if on no other (ibid, p. 207).

The New Left and the Old Left

When the proposals came to the Annual Conference, the misunderstandings about the nature of the new proposals came to the fore. Most of the points of policy were accepted including the NEB and the Planning Agreements. However, the mixed economy basis of the nationalisation programme escaped the old left or, alternatively, they realised the implications only too well.

In the Conference Arrangements Committee, the compositing necessary to produce a reasonable number of resolutions for discussion resulted in the proposal to nationalise 25 top companies having added to it the idea that this should be a first step towards nationalising 250 monopolies with minimum compensation. The two local branches involved in this amendment were Brighton Kemp Town, closely associated with the Militant tendency, a trotskyist group, and Eric Heffer's constituency, Liverpool Walton (ibid, pp. 217-218). The original motion would almost certainly have been carried easily but the final extravaganza was thrown out. In the debate Wilson tried to pacify the left by offering more nationalisations. However, he was clearly anxious to avoid commitments regarding manufacturing concerns and offered more basic industries (shipbuilding and ship repairing) and infrastructure (docks). He was offering exactly what the "new left" didn't want; more loss leaders without growth potential (all the industries mentioned were in serious financial straits) and unable to exercise any competitive influence on the private sector (ibid, p. 213; p. 220).

The growing strength of the "new left" was now apparent despite the conference setbacks. It had a programme, it was gaining influence in the party and it had forced the dominant social democratic group in the party hierarchy into a debate in which the latter had initially conceded much of the argument and had been forced into a defensive position from which they had little to offer in terms of policy which might prevent a recurence of the intellectual and political disasters of 1964-1970.

Crosland's Reply

Crosland, however, set to work on a major reply to Holland, the result of which was the essay "Socialism Now" published in the latter half of 1973. While admitting the central failure of Labour's economic policy during the last government, he challenged Holland's central concept of a shift of power from the state to multi-national companies. Without disputing the growing concentration in industry, he concluded that this was more than offset by the growing share of government in GNP (now 49%) and investment (41% of domestic fixed capital formation in 1972) and the growing power of the trade unions. He was also able to point to the high level of new controls imposed on private capital by the Heath Government after the by-now famous U-turn (Crosland, 1975, pp. 28-29). He also suggested that if the analysis of Glyn and Sutcliffe were correct (Glyn and Sutcliffe, 1972), then British capitalism was literally fighting for its life as its profits plummeted, its markets disappeared and in the face of a workers offensive. He also argued that nationalising 25 of the top 100 companies would only give the government control of about 4% of GNP. Manufacturing was now only a third of GNP, such had been the switch to services in the past decade (Crosland, 1975(a), p. 29-30). In his opinion, the failure of investment and exports were the result of government policy. Deflation had destroyed final demand at home and weakened the competitive base. He had nothing to say about the growing export of capital and transfer of manufacturing overseas by British companies but argued that the British experience of decline was not paralleled elsewhere in the Western World and therefore was of domestic origin (ibid, p. 33).

He went on to argue quite rightly that Holland's proposals were based on French bureaucratic elitism masquerading as socialism and also that Weber was more relevant than Marx in considering the question of the concentration of power. For good measure he drew attention to the lack of democratic responsibility and popular control in the nationalised industries and suggested a halt be called to further nationalisation proposals until these problems had been tackled in the existing state sector (ibid, pp. 34-35). Two of his most weighty criticisms, however, were that nationalisation with adequate compensation, which was being proposed, could do nothing to change the imbalance of wealth in society, the correction of which he considered now one of Labour's prime tasks and to remedy which he now proposed the nationalisation of land (ibid, p. 13), nor resolve the growing problem of the supply of management (ibid, pp. 35-36). However, having made a substantial critique of Holland's case, he went on to call for "an active policy of competitive public enterprise". Britain needed a State Holding Company and a State Investment Bank as "a responsible agency for the conduct of selective intervention". He added "(t)his is a fresher and more attractive approach than the old one. It moves us away from monolithic industry nationalisation towards nationalisation by company". As this was exactly what Holland and now Benn were proposing, it is clear that the differences between Crosland and the new left were differences on the scale and degree of state intervention now needed rather than the type of intervention itself. It was a debate between the right and left wings of social democracy to the exclusion of traditional socialist reformism but, as the Conference fiasco had indicated, the latter was still around and kicking.

While the two wings of social democracy had been engaged in this wide debate, the men who would dominate the party in the next government - Wilson, Callaghan and Healey - had not played any leading role. In fact, as Wilson's speech at the Conference showed, he really had not grasped the significance of the debate at all for his proposals were at odds with both sides in the previous arguments (Hatfield, 1978, pp. 219-220). Callaghan had played no small role in the reconcilation of unions with party which would stand him in good stead on Wilson's resignation, but had contributed little on economic issues. However, the party approached the next election with a far more radical programme than for years, and with the fall of the Heath Government before a miner's strike, found itself back in government within 6 months.

4.
SOCIAL DEMOCRACY ABANDONED: THE LABOUR GOVERNMENT 1974-1979

If the 1964-1970 Labour Government represented the failure of social democracy to cope with economic difficulties, the 1974-79 government was in terms of social democracy, whether of the right or left variety, a total disaster. Not only did this period see more economic failure, this time on a far grander scale, but also the formal abandonment of the social demo- cratic commitment to full employment and increased social welfare and the abandonment, again formally, of its Keynesian underpinnings and assumptions. No one should doubt the constraints, external and internal, that the government faced, but nor should they doubt that almost every economic response of the government was away from social democracy and towards an orthodox conservative approach to economic crisis. By the end of its period of office it was clear that the government had no policy except to ride out the crisis. Labour Party economic policy was back to the pre-Keynesian position.

Elected in February 1974 with manifesto pledges "to bring about a fundamental and irreversible shift in the balance of power and wealth in favour of the working people and their families,...to make power in industry genuinely accountable to the workers and the community at large,...(and) to increase social equality by giving far greater importance to full employ- ment, housing, education and social benefits..." (Times, 9.2.74, pp. 4-5), the Labour Government found itself immediately in difficulties. It was the first post-war minority government with a deficit of 33 seats against all other parties. Labour had polled only 37.2% of the vote, its lowest share since 1931 and had in fact polled some 260,000 votes less than the Conservatives, gaining more seats only on the vagaries of the first-past- the-post-system. It had lost 6% of the overall vote since 1970 in a swing towards minority parties, which had gained almost 25% of the vote, the Liberals 19.3%, and 37 seats (Guardian Weekly, 9.3.74, pp. 1-5). The indecisive result clearly meant another election within months. As a result, the first months of the new government were uneventful. Denis Healey, the new Chancellor, presented a moderately redistributive budget, increasing old age pensions, food and housing subsidies, and raising taxes on cigarettes, drink and higher incomes. His budget also prefigured wealth and gift taxes for the future (New Statesman, 29.3.74, pp. 429- 431). Benn was re-appointed Minister of Industry and was to draft proposals for Labour's industry policy assisted by Eric Heffer, Michael Meacher and Stuart Holland (Hatfield, 1978, p. 230; p. 232). Ominously, however, for Labour's new policy, Benn was the only cabinet member associated with the programme. When the new election was called for October, a New Statesman editorial noted "There has been one act which can be wholeheartedly welcomed...and that is the repeal of the industrial relations legislation. Otherwise, it has been a blank, not to say bleak, six months" (New Statesman, 6.9.74, p. 301).

In the run up to the October election, Shirley Williams announced she would withdraw from public life if the referendum on the EEC to which Labour was committed decided against membership. Roy Jenkins also announced that he would not remain in the cabinet in the event of a "no" vote. These pronouncements undoubtedly cost Labour votes (Wilson, 1979,

p. 83) and the result was little better than February's, although Labour now had a wafer-thin majority of 3. However, its overall vote was lower than in February and it owed its "success" to the fact that the Conservatives had lost 1.5million votes between the two elections. Minority parties still held 25% of the vote (Guardian Weekly, 19.10.74, p. 3). During its term the majority of 3 evaporated as the result of by-election defeats and in 1977 the government was forced to enter into an agreement with the Liberals to avoid an early election. Therefore throughout its life the government was constrained by the lack of a working majority.

Against this background of electoral impasse the economy had continued to deteriorate. Labour had inherited from Mr. Heath, the "three day week", rising inflation, a declining currency, the pound now "floating", and a massive trade deficit. By the end of 1974, inflation was above 20% p.a., while GNP had fallen 2.5%, unemployment had reached 1 million, and the trade deficit was 3350 million pounds, a record (Coates, 1980, p. 8; pp. 11-12). Externally, as a result of the oil crisis, industrial production fell world-wide by ten per cent and intra-metropolitan trade was reduced by 13% in 1974: the biggest crash since 1929 (Glyn and Harrison, 1980, pp. 18-23). Any attempt to resolve the internal crisis would have to cope with external constraints.

The Election Programme Abandoned

The Queen's speech following the October election contained plans for the NEB, planning agreements, a public trustee to step into failing companies, and plans for workers participation in management. However, the cabinet had already reduced the planning agreements and NEB national-isations to a voluntary basis and by the time the Industry Act was published in January 1975, the provisions for compulsory disclosures had vanished as had plans for a public trustee (Hatfield, 1980, pp. 238-239; p. 241). By now Denis Healey was attacking the proposals as inflationary and demanding a deflationary policy (ibid, pp. 235-236) and the Confederation of British Industry had announced "there was absolutely no room for compromise or negotiation about further state intervention in industry and further nationalisation". The glass giant, Pilkington's, let it be known that their entire investment programme, worth 150 million pounds, was suspended "until such time as essential changes are made in taxation and price control", a fairly blatant threat of a strike of capital (Glyn and Harrison, 1980, p. 104).

That was really the end of Labour's new programme. The NEB was set up but its new task was to take care of bankrupt companies bailed out by the government. Commenting in the Washington Post, Bernard Nossiter noted "the NEB has been transformed from a socialist beehive into a capitalist nursing home" (Washington Post reprinted in Guardian Weekly, 14.3.76, p. 17) and the only planning agreement signed was with the National Coal Board, a nationalised industry (Wilson, 1979, p. 141). The policy was abandoned almost without a whimper by a cabinet that had never supported it in the first place. Benn, with whom the policy had now become firmly associated in the party and the public's mind, was removed from the Ministry of Industry in the wake of the EEC referendum's "yes" vote for continued membership against which Benn and most of the left had campaigned. He was transferred to Energy but without responsibility for North Sea Oil. Despite a backbench revolt, Wilson's strength in the Parlia-mentary Party was sufficient for him to effectively neutralise Benn

(Hatfield, 1978, pp. 247-249). While the "new left" had won the intellectual debate in the party at large in the years of opposition, it had made little progress in the Parliamentary Party. This complete cabinet about face almost within days of the election goes a long way towards explaining the current near obsession of the "new left" with the accountability of the parliamentary party. However, having abandoned its economic programme, the Labour Government was faced with how to cope with the most serious economic crisis since the war both in Britain and in the world at large, and having abandoned a revamped social democratic programme, it began to move away from social democracy altogether.

Deflation Again

Having abandoned plans for greater intervention in industry, the Government was without a policy and the situation it was facing made a neo-Keynesian response problematic. Inflation, unemployment and the balance of trade deficit were all rising at the same time; something the neo-Keynesian paradigm, which concentrated almost exclusively on demand management, suggested was highly unlikely if not impossible. Keynes himself did not go as far as his later followers in this. He certainly saw inflation as being a possibility at less than full employment and his concern with long-term profit levels and investment volumes suggest that this is exactly what he thought would eventuate if major income redistribution and investment planning were not instituted. However, by far the most forceful statement of the possibilities of inflationary stagnation had been from the Polish economist Michael Kalecki who had arrived independently at similar conclusion to Keynes during the depression of the 1930s (Keynes, 1973, pp. 163-164; pp. 301-304; Kalecki, 1943). If demand was increased to reduce unemployment, inflation and the balance of trade deficit would almost certainly rise. If demand was reduced, unemployment would rise. Healey's November budget gave 1.5 billion pounds to industry, reduced price controls and corporation tax, but also reduced government expenditure by 2% p.a. for the next four years and threatened the trade unions with massive unemployment resulting from deflationary policies if wage claims were not moderated. (Taylor, 1978, p. 309). His April 1975 budget, however, was highly deflationary: VAT was increased, income tax was raised from 33% to 35% and government expenditure was cut by a further one billion pounds in the current year, with plans for three billion pounds in cuts for 1976. All commentators were agreed the budget was certain to raise unemployment and alone had added almost 3% to inflation (Guardian Weekly, 19.4.75). By August, unemployment had reached 1.25 million, the highest figure since 1945, and Healey was warning of "two to three million on the dole for years" at a trade union rally (Guardian Weekly, 26.7.75, p. 3; ibid, 30.8.75, p. 3). But it was not just Wilson and Healey who were abandoning the party's commitment to full employment as government policy, undoubtedly one of the main planks of both social democratic and Keynesian thinking.

Full Circle: The Abandonment of Keynes

In an editorial at the beginning of the year, entitled "A Year For Realities", the social democratic journal, Socialist Commentary, with which many of the party's leading social democrats had been associated for many years, noted:

> In 1975, the most important impacts on the lives of
> the people of this country will be the consequence
> of what happens in the rest of the world. What we
> do ourselves will be significant more as a reaction
> to and an attempt to cope with these outside
> events and forces, than as representing any kind of
> unfettered national will or initiative...
>
> It seems clear to us that in 1975, the level of
> employment in this country will be almost entirely
> beyond the control of the British Government. It
> will be determined mainly by trends in the world
> economy that affect our exports, and by world
> financial developments that affect our ability to
> substitute higher home demand for any drop in
> export demand (Socialist Commentary, Jan. 1975,
> pp. 1-2).

It is difficult to imagine any statement that could depart much further from Keynesian thinking. Undoubtedly, Britain faced a crisis of major proportions, but the essence of the Keynesian revolution was in combatting external pressures towards slump by controlling the domestic situation; by keeping the domestic economy going rather than bowing to the inevitability of the external constraints. Another article in the same issue entitled "Socialist Money is Sound Money" argued that the Treasury was right in insisting sound money was an essential background for steady progress with redistribution. The author was Joan Mitchell, Shirley Williams' personal economic advisor at the Department of Prices and Consumer Affairs (ibid, pp. 4-5). The left's response on the other hand was undoubtedly Keynesian; they added import controls to their programme (ibid, March 1975, p. 1-2). Throughout 1975, unemployment continued to rise, reaching just under 1.5 million by the end of the year (Guardian Weekly, 1.2.76, p. 1; p. 3). In the summer of 1975 Healey had imposed a ten percent limit on wage increases with a maximum of six pounds. It was clear by now that the government was treating wages as the major problem and seeking to remedy it by the use of unemployment and new statutory controls. While wages had been rising faster than inflation since the election, the reason was evident. Because of the increased burden of taxation falling on the wage earner and particularly wage earners with families, wage increases limited to RPI indexes were insufficient to keep up purchasing power (Incidently, probably the major factor in the current wage push inflation in Australia). A ten percent wage increase does not provide 10% net, because the failure to index tax allowances means that any increase in wages carries a standard rate tax burden. The problem can be vividly illustrated by the movement of tax thresholds relative to the average wage:

Table 5: Tax Thresholds as a % of the Average Wage

	1963/64	1969/70	1972/73	1976/77
Couple with 2 children	84.5%	56.1%	59.9%	47.1%
Couple with 4 children	125.8%	75.6%	78.9%	63.0%

(Source: Field, 1979, p. 32).

Therefore any attempt to hold wages to inflation means a wage cut and Mr. Healey's six pound limit was undoubtedly that. This was put forward as a voluntary agreement: the TUC did agree but Healey had already announced the policy was statutory for the public sector and that companies would not be able to pass on any excess in higher prices. The attack on wages also came at a time when UK wages were by far the lowest in Western Europe, being half of West German rates and two-thirds of even Italian rates (Washington Post, reprinted Guardian Weekly, 13.6.76, p. 16).

By the beginning of 1976, it was clear that not only had the social democrats abandoned Keynesianism but that they had also swallowed the monetarist package. A Socialist Commentary editorial entitled "Prices First, Not Jobs" declared:

> During 1976 there is a first priority for British economic policy, and that is to bring down the rate of inflation. There is a second priority...the improvement of productivity...And there is a third priority, reducing unemployment, which can be tackled only when we have beaten inflation, and only by measures that do not obstruct the improvement of productivity...There is nothing that can be done this year about the hundreds of thousands that would be needed to reduce unemployment meaningfully. It is more likely to increase...(Socialist Commentary, Jan. 1976, pp. 1-2).

The monetarist, Mrs. Thatcher, now Leader of the Conservatives, could not have put it better. It was also not as if the inflation was entirely due to excess demand: the savings ratio, itself a deflationary factor, was at an all time high at 14.3% of GNP as a result of high interest rates (Frances Cairncross, Guardian Weekly, 4.4.76, p. 6) and many price increases resulted from the continuing decline in the value of the pound.

In February 1976, Healey announced further public expenditure cuts in education, housing and transport of 2.4 billion pounds. However, government spending still continued to rise to meet increased debt interest resulting from high interest rates (Guardian Weekly, 29.2.76, pp. 3-4), a problem that would beset Mrs. Thatcher's attempts to reduce state spending after 1979 in the context of a monetarist strategy.

In March 1976, as the result of a failed Bank of England attempt to secure a small reduction in the parity of the currency, a run on the pound began that did not end until the IMF intervened at the end of the year and granted the UK a loan of $3.9 billion, the largest ever negotiated. The pound broke the $2.00 barrier in March and by October had reached $1.60. A further deflationary package was announced in July 1976, which included further public expenditure cuts of one billion pounds and increased taxes by another one billion pounds by imposing a 2% surcharge on National Insurance Contributions. On 29th September 1976, the government asked the IMF to intervene (Sunday Times, 14.5.78, pp. 33-35). A few days before James Callaghan, now Prime Minister following Wilson's resignation in March, addressed the Party Conference and not only rejected Keynesian solutions to the crisis, but in fact blamed Keynesianism for the crisis itself:

> We used to think that you could just spend your way
> out of a recession and increase employment by
> cutting taxes and boosting Government spending. I
> tell you in all candour that that option no longer
> exists and insofar as it ever did exist, it worked by
> injecting inflation into the economy. And each
> time that happened the average level of
> unemployment has risen. Higher inflation followed
> by higher unemployment. That is the history of the
> last twenty years (James Callaghan cited
> Beckerman 1979, p. 50).

He forgot to mention that the 50s and early 60s, the heyday of neo-Keynesianism, were marked by economic growth, high employment and negligible inflation.

The IMF Intervention

The IMF's recipe was a $1.50 pound and another 4 billion pounds cut in public spending. Belatedly even Callaghan baulked at the scale and took over control of the negotiations from Healey. He threatened to withdraw the British Army from Germany, to end sterling's role as a reserve currency thereby putting pressure on the dollar, and told the IMF the alternative to concessions was Benn (Sunday Times, 21.5.78, pp. 33-34) but later gave in as he had no alternative economic policy. In the cabinet at first there was a clear majority against further spending cuts. An alliance of the social democrats, Benn and the old left outnumbered the Callaghan-Healey forces. It is reported that Crosland and Hattersley seriously considered the AES as preferable to the IMF terms. However, not all the social democrats agreed and it was defeated. Crosland then fell back on import controls but by now he was isolated from the social democratic group in cabinet. Jenkins supported the IMF terms, Rodgers did not favour increased public spending and Williams and Lever opposed any form of protectionism, which did not altogether square with their near obsessive support for the EEC, which is certainly a protectionist block. Crosland was now faced with an alliance with the left or capitulation. He chose the latter as far as can be established because he knew a revolt at that time meant the end of the government and an election at which Labour would be annihilated (Sunday Times, 28.5.78, p. 34; Hattersley, 1981, p. 10). This finally produced Crosland's break with the social democrats. Crosland died in February 1977 of a heart attack but in his last months insisted on calling himself a democratic socialist and describing a social democrat as "somebody about to join the Tory Party" (Peter Jenkins, Guardian Weekly, 27.2.77, p. 5; Bell, 1977, p. 90). In January 1977, Roy Jenkins had quit politics to join the EEC as Commissioner so within two months, the social democrats had lost their two leading figures in Parliament. With Callaghan's acceptance in principal of the IMF terms, the latter compromised and public expenditure cuts of 2.5 billion pounds over 2 years were agreed (Sunday Times, 28.5.78, pp. 33-34).

In December 1976, the Manifesto Group, the PLP social democratic group issued a statement "What We Must Do" claiming that inflation was still the first priority and supporting cuts in government spending (Socialist Commentary, Jan. 1977, pp. 3-5).

Thereafter, the Labour Government eked out an existence until 1979 when it suffered a catastrophic defeat at the hands of Mrs. Thatcher. It's final months in office were marked by serious industrial strife as workers broke out of the pay straitjacket imposed by Healey and sought to regain their purchasing power.

The Balance Sheet

Crosland's opposition to further spending cuts in 1976 was clearly based on the Keynesian premise that in an economy already suffering from excess capacity, spending cuts and further deflation could only prolong or even intensify the recession. This was certainly the case as it transpired. Undoubtedly inflation fell and the balance of payments improved but industrial production fell by 7%, not regaining even the level of Mr. Heath's "three day week" until 1978/79, and unemployment held steady at 1.5 million (Glyn and Harrison, 1980, pp. 118-122; Coates, 1980, p. 46). Glyn and Harrison estimate that the fall in real wages in the period 1976-78, some 8%, was the highest since the mid-nineteenth century. The whole structure of state spending had changed, with unemployment pay and debt interest now taking the lion's share, while housing, education and health failed to maintain the levels of 1973-74, never mind Labour's 1974 proposals (Glyn and Harrison, 1980, p. 121) and public investment was more than 20% below 1975-76 levels (Owen, 1981, p. 137). At the same time as the social wage was reduced the burden of taxation on the lower paid continued to rise:

Table 6: Direct Taxation as a % of Income

	May 1973	May 1979	% Increase
on half average earnings	8	12	50%
on average earnings	21	25	19%
on twice average earnings	26	30	15%
on 5 times average earnings	37	50	35%

(Source: The Economist, 14.3.81, pp. 33-34).

After the election the party was in tatters. Perhaps the biggest blow was to its ethos: committed to full employment it had presided over the highest unemployment since the war and more importantly had clearly used unemployment as a tool of economc policy. Its commitment to the welfare state was no longer clear, while the burden of the state itself was now a major cause of poverty. In 1979, it was difficult to see what was left of the social democratic consensus outlined by Crosland more than 20 years previously. And more importantly in the retreat to fiscal conservatism the social democrats and the new left for that matter had been sunk almost without trace. Many had remained in office including Williams, Owen and Rodgers as had Benn, but none had had any influence on a policy, dominated by Callaghan, Healey and the Treasury. However, in Benn's case he had at least proposed an alternative policy whereas the others had gone along with the policies of Callaghan and Healey and even their continued commitment to social democratic policies was somewhat open to question.

In case it should be thought that conversion to monetarism was a British disease in the context of socialist parties, it should be remembered that by far the hardest line of the question of the IMF loan to Britain was taken by Helmut Schmidt of the SPD who repeatedly spoke on the need to extirpate the Keynesian heresy and whom both Callaghan and Wilson described as somewhere to the right of Milton Friedman in their discussions at the European Council (Sunday Times, 28.5.78, p. 33; Wilson, 1979, p. 237).

5.
THE LEGACY OF CALLAGHAN AND HEALEY

The election of 1979 was a debacle for Labour. With less than 37% of the vote and only just 28% of the electorate, it was Labour's worst post-war performance. The Conservatives had polled over 2 million more votes than Labour in an election which had seen third party votes fall back from 25% of the poll in 1974 to about 19%. Despite this, Labour's vote was even lower than 1974, its previous low point. In 1951, the Labour vote had been almost 14 million, its highest ever. In 1979, it polled just over 11 million in an electorate swollen by 5 million more voters (Guardian Weekly, 13.5.79, p. 6; Stewart 1974, p. 130). But even these figures concealed worse realities for Labour. An opinion poll published in the New Statesman, which gave a very accurate prediction of the final result, showed that even among manual workers, Labour's traditional constituency, less than half would vote Labour: 47% against 43% for the Conservatives. The poll suggested there had been a 15% swing from Labour to the Conservatives in this group since 1974. This was confirmed by another poll by the MORI Organisation on election day which also found that only 50% of trade unionists had voted for Labour (New Statesman, 6.4.79, pp. 470-471; ibid, 18.5.79, pp. 704-705); ample evidence that the Wilson and Callaghan governments had led to the disintegration of much of Labour's traditional support.

However, of far greater importance was the damage the party had done to its own ethos. It had abandoned its commitment to full employment and had for over four years pursued a policy of orthodox fiscal conservatism, using unemployment as a tool in the fight against inflation, in defence of the currency, and to remedy a balance of payments deficit. It had almost been a repeat performance of the 1929-31 Government of Ramsay MacDonald and Phillip Snowden. In fact at the December 1976 cabinet meeting to discuss the IMF package, Benn had only stopped a move to cut unemployment pay by circulating copies of the fateful 1931 cabinet meeting minutes, where the very narrow majority for the proposal had led to MacDonald and Snowden quitting Labour to form the National Government in alliance with the Conservatives (Sunday Times, 28.5.78, p. 36). As early as 1978 the Cambridge Economic Policy Group had warned that unemployment would top 2 million in 1981, 3 million by 1985 and 5 million by the end of the decade unless government policies changed (Beckerman, 1979, p. 61). All the traditions of the party, Socialism, Social Democracy and even Keynesianism, had been abandoned in the rush back to "monetarism" and pre-Keynesian economics. The party could not claim that these policies had been forced on them by the IMF or by the parliamentary pact with the Liberals in 1977 for as has been shown in the previous chapter, the policy change had been decided upon, in theory and in practice, long before the IMF intervention late in 1976. The IMF demands were merely another turn of the screw. And neither was the policy solely the work of Wilson, Callaghan and Healey. Many of the old social democratic wing of the party were equally committed to these policies and many of the old left including the new deputy leader, Michael Foot had gone along with them. Shirley Williams was the government's staunchest defender on the NEC, and in the pre-election budget discussions, she and William Rodgers were among the most vigorous of those endorsing further cash spending limits on government departments (Peter Jenkins, Guardian Weekly, 4.3.79, p. 10; New Statesman, 19.3.79, p. 74-75). To the embarrassment of the party, on the eve of the election, figures published by the European Commission indicated that the UK's public spending rate was the second lowest in the EEC (New Statesman, 11.5.79, p. 667). The New Statesman's, post-election editorial, "The Choice Labour Faces: Learn or Die" said openly what many Labour supporters secretly thought:

> ...there are worse things than electoral reverse. Another five years of office, of the imposition of half-Tory measures cloaked in half-socialist rhetoric, would most likely have assured the demolition of the Labour coalition...That is still a worse prospect for Britain that any damage the Tories are likely to inflict (11.5.79, p. 666).

The same editorial also warned that a catastrophe under the Conservatives would be as likely to produce an upsurge of support for the Liberals as a return to Labour, such was Labour's spoiled image. The New Statesman is by no means a supporter of the Labour left and their editorial comment gives an indication of the depth of disillusionment felt by the movement.

In office, the Thatcher Government tightened the monetary screws, raised interest rates to new peaks, Minimum Lending Rate to 17%, announced further cuts in government spending, doubled VAT to 15% while making marginal cuts in income tax rates (Guardian Weekly, 17.6.79, p. 1). Not very different from the policies pursued by the Callaghan-Healey Government, but again one more turn of the screw. The only change was the dropping of the corporatist appendage: the attempt to tie the trade unions to the policy through statutory and voluntary income policies. Meanwhile Labour's post-election shadow cabinet showed few changes from government. Healey topped the poll for the 12 elected positions. Of the 12 only one, Peter Shore had been associated with continued opposition to the IMF terms. The leading social democrats elected were Hattersley, Rodgers and Owen. Shirley Williams having lost her seat at the election with an above average swing against her (Guardian Weekly, 24.6.79, p. 5; 13.5.79, p. 6). Benn refused to stand. As for the position of the social democrats in the Labour Party, the Guardian Journalist, Peter Jenkins commented:

> For the time being the social democrats in the Labour Party are generals without a strategy, an elite without a cause. Their programme is in tatters but they continue to preside ,(Guardian Weekly, 4.3.79, p. 10).

Jenkins' comments are important for since the social democratic split got under way in August 1980, he has been their foremost champion in the press. Not surprisingly, Labour's performance in opposition was negligible. By the end of August, another New Statesman editorial was entitled "Callaghan must go".

It read:

> Callaghan has turned out to be an even worse
> leader of the opposition than he was a Prime
> Minister. As the Tories press on with their
> strategy of denuding the social and industrial
> landscape, the electors could be forgiven for not
> noticing any coherent on energetic Labour
> response...Partly this is because the policy options
> of the last government very often held the door
> open to charges of "you too". But equally it is
> because Callaghan perceives the real enemy as
> being the National Executive (and much of the
> membership) of his own party (24.8.79, p. 259).

The position of the left since the election defeat has also changed
from what it had been after the 1970 defeat. Then it had concerned itself
with theory and policy, now it was mainly concerned with questions of
organisation in particular with the accountability of the leadership and the
parliamentary party (Guardian Weekly, 30.9.79, p. 5). This was hardly
surprising, having clearly won the debate in the early 1970s, having had
most of its ideas and practical policies included in both the election manifestos of 1974, the problem was not, as they saw it to bring forward new
policies, but rather to see how they could ensure that the already agreed
policies be implemented by future governments. In this they were joined by
some of the most influential trade union leaders, in particular
David Basnett (GMWU), Moss Evans (TGWU) and Clive Jenkins (ASTMS). In
fact, rather as they had done after the electoral disaster of 1931, the trade
unions moved towards taking greater control of the Labour Party
(Peter Jenkins Guardian Weekly, 5.10.80, p. 4). At the October
Conference, a decision was made for an enquiry into the structure of the
party, in particular it was to consider the election of future party leaders,
the control of future election manifestos, and the reselection of sitting
MPs. As the parliamentary party had virtually total control of the first
two and reselection of MPs was automatic, the enquiry represented a
threat to the autonomy and authority of the parliamentary party. Probably
the final straw for the trade unions, who were by no stretch of imagination
to be identified with the left, was that Callaghan and Healey blamed them
for the election defeat. While, undoubtedly, the strikes of the "winter of
discontent" did not help Labour's re-election chances, it is indisputable that
the major reason for the defeat was the mass desertion of traditional
Labour voters which had been apparent since 1977 (Patrick Wintour and
Francis Wheen, New Statesman, 5.10.79, pp. 492-493). In fact the Labour
vote recovered in 1979. The right's opposition was heard very little.
Mainly it consisted of misrepresenting the left's case for greater involve-
ment in the economy, mainly for the benefit of the press who were only too
anxious to repeat it. Typical was Healey's outburst just before the Conference in defense of the mixed economy which he turned into an attack on
Benn. As the mixed economy was not in dispute it was clearly pure
bluster. On the Conference eve, The Guardian journalist, Peter Jenkins,
summed up the plight of the right and the social democrats:

> Mr. Callaghan's weak position has three causes. He
> lost the election...His power base in the trade
> unions has been eroded...The third reason however
> is the most important. The right wing of the
> Labour Party has passed into the hands of the
> ideological receiver; intellectually it is bankrupt
> (Guardian Weekly, 7.10.79, p. 10).

Jenkins admitted that the social democrats had failed because of their inability to operate the mixed economy effectively and as a result the centre ground has collapsed beneath them. He did not believe the West German SPD model was valid because the negative power of the trade unions in the UK was too great but warned that the major threat to freedom came not from the left but from the danger "that persistent and worsening economic failure will eventually undermine our free institutions" (ibid). At the Conference itself, the left now clearly led by Benn and his supporters in the local parties carried all before them. The alternative economic strategy, unilateral nuclear disarmament, a motion to leave the EEC and the accountability of the leadership were all carried easily.

Thus the political implications of the Wilson-Callaghan years were becoming starker. The electoral base was being eroded, the two most important party constituents, the trade unions and the constituency parties were in revolt. But at the same time an entrenched parliamentary party was devoid of ideas. It could neither oppose the Thatcher government's monetarist experiment nor offer any effective intellectual opposition to the left in the party at large. Without doubt the party now faced its gravest post-war crisis, which perhaps it should have faced in 1976 but which had been postponed. However, it was now clear the problems had come home to roost. This became abundantly obvious in July 1980 when the NEC released a draft party manifesto in line with the previous year's Conference decisions. The Shadow Cabinet disowned it and cancelled the press conference at which it was to be launched. This was despite a 1979 Conference decision that future manifestos were the responsibility of the NEC (Times, 11.7.80, p. 1).

6.
THE SPLIT: THE IMMEDIATE CAUSES AND THE UNDERLYING CAUSES

The Immediate Causes of Contention

On the 1st August 1980, David Owen, William Rodgers and Shirley Williams published an open letter to the Labour Party in The Guardian. Recognising that the Labour Party faced the greatest crisis in its history, the letter went on to list three items on which it considered there was no room for equivocation in the Party; commitment to the mixed economy, commitment to a truly international socialism and an "unshakable" commitment to representative democracy. As I have argued in previous chapters, the question of the "mixed economy" was not now seriously challenged by the left unless it was to be defined very narrowly as the status quo. As for international socialism as defined in the document, it amounted to a commitment to the Third World, to the EEC and to NATO. Notwithstanding the obvious contradiction between support for a protectionist bloc like the EEC and trade with the Third World, it would not have been unreasonable to ask what had been the Wilson and Callaghan Governments' commitments to the Third World, which were now so threatened by the left's demands for import controls. As for internationalism and NATO, it is hard to see the connection. But by far the largest section was devoted to the question of representative democracy. What concerned "the Three" was the growing demands for accountability of the party's elected representatives:

> For decades debates on policy and on organisation have gone on within our party and we have managed to find some way of working together. But this time the far left want no compromise. It is seeking not only to dominate the party but to destroy representative democracy itself. MPs are chosen by their constituents to exercise their consciences and judgement. MPs or councillors, who are nothing but mandated party delegates cannot be representatives of their constituencies in the true sense. They cease to be accountable to the people who elected them and become instead rubber stamps for a party caucus, one that does not even include the majority of party members (The Guardian, 1.8.80, p. 11, emphasis added).

Here I would argue is one of the most immediate causes of the "Social Democrat's" split from the Party. It is often not appreciated outside of Britain just how much autonomy the Parliamentary Party, and Labour Local Councils for that matter, have had. Clause V of the Party Constitution lays down that party manifestos shall be decided by the Parliamentary Party and the NEC together. However, if they fail to agree then the Prime Minister and the Parliamentary Party decide the manifesto. Thus the parliamentary Party can veto any party policy not to its liking merely by refusing to agree (M. Thomas, The Times, 15.1.81, p. 10). This is quite beyond the question of the Party in government ignoring or ever adopting policies diametrically opposed to those on which it was elected once in office as it has repeatedly done. The Party as a whole had no sanction over the parliamentary group short of withholding funds and bringing the whole organisation to its knees. This lack of accountability may work in good times when the system is capable of delivering higher living standards, but it will not survive in hard times when the abject failure of the party to deliver on its election promises or even to show reasonable competence in office in line with its aims becomes obvious. This is what happened in 1931 and it was happening again in 1980. The party as a whole was calling its elected representatives to order. What also has to be said about the open letter's plea for the autonomy of the "conscience and judgement" of elected representatives is that it is very much an argument against the party system itself.

'The Three''s views on party democracy have subsequently become a little clearer with the leaking of the proposed constitution for the SDP drafted by David Owen. It is proposed that 'members of the party are to be consulted on the formation of party policy, both nationally and locally, by means of postal questionnaires, at least once a year' (New Statesman, 3.4.81, p. 4). This sort of system which envisages no policy-making role for conferences leaves the centre holding all the cards, with resources, finance and information at its disposal. An active political membership as opposed to an electoral machine is therefore quite clearly seen as an encumberance to an elite leadership exercising their consciences and judgement. Here we have the crux of their problem. With little or no support in the constituency parties or the trade unions the only way they could continue as before was on the basis of their "autonomy" from any form of party control. And now that was reduced if not removed.

That 'the Three' were stating their terms for remaining in the party was made emminently clear:

> If the NEC remains committed to pursuing its present course and if, consequently, fears multiply among the people, then support for a centre party will strengthen as disaffected voters move away from Labour. We have already said that we will not support a centre party for it would lack roots and a coherent philosophy. But if the Labour Party abandons its democratic and internationalist principles, the argument may grow for a new democratic socialist party to establish itself as a party of conscience and reform committed to those principles. We are not prepared to abandon Britain to divisive and often cruel Tory policies because electors do not have an opportunity to vote for an acceptable socialist alternative to a Conservative Government (Guardian, 1.8.80, p. 11).

What was to some extent surprising was that despite the claim of the open letter that the Party's policies were electorally unacceptable, 'the Three''s challenge came at a time when the Party was enjoying greater electoral popularity that for years. In the May 1980 local government elections Labour had kept or gained control of nearly 80% of Britain's cities (Guardian Weekly, 11.5.80, p. 3) and also at a time when all the evidence pointed to Callaghan being able to make a deal with the trade union leaders to resist many of the left's demands for constitutional changes (ibid, 29.6.80, p. 5). However, by the Conference the trade union leaders' position had hardened, whether in response to 'the Three''s ultimatum is not at all clear, and major constitutional changes were proposed and passed. All MPs were in future to be subject to a reselection procedure and future leaders of the Party were to be elected by an electoral college representing the party as a whole. On policy issues the Conference voted for the Alternative Economic Strategy, import controls, withdrawal from the EEC, unilateral nuclear disarmament and the closing of US bases in Britain. Surprisingly, the Party voted overwhelmingly to remain in NATO. It also refused to give the NEC control of future election manifestos and kept the status quo ﹒ (Times, 2.10.80, p. 1; 3.10.80, p. 1; p. 4). What is clear is that none of the policies voted by the Conference are of themselves incompatible with social democracy. With the exception of import controls one is rather reminded of the Swedish and Austrian social democratic parties considered by many to be models of moderation. As for the electoral liability of this programme, it has to be remembered that most of these policies had been voted by Conference for many years past and Labour had been elected twice on similar programmes in 1974. Without doubt, the organisational changes were the immediate point at issue. In particular, the reselection of MPs would mean that in future MPs and even Ministers out of line with party policy were liable to be thrown out by local constituency activists. There was no evidence that any of the leading social democrats were immediately threatened but the possibility was there for the future.

Immediately following the Conference, Callaghan announced his resignation. The obvious successor in the parliamentary Party was Healey. However, despite his initial reluctance, Michael Foot was persuaded by the trade union leaders to stand. It was clearly a 'stop Healey' move as one leading trade unionist admitted "If we cannot stop him, we can control his bloody arrogance" following TUC talks on the subject﹒ (Times, 21.10,80, p. 1). Despite Healey being a clear favourite, Foot was elected on the second ballot by 139 votes to 129 (Times, 11.11.80, p. 1) in a vote which many MPs interpreted as a wish for a quiet life on the part of MPs in the belief that Foot could restore a measure of unity to the party as a whole while a vote for Healey could have meant a major clash with the unions and the local parties on policy questions. The Parliamentary Party had retained the right to elect the leader until the exact form of the future electoral college had been decided by a special conference.

'The Three' and their co-thinkers must have been in a dilemma. While they may have agreed with Healey on most policy issues there was no greater champion of parliamentary privilege and the autonomy of the Parliamentary Party than Michael Foot. His interview in New Left Review when he was still on the backbenches can leave no doubt of that (Foot 1968, p. 31), nor can his record as Leader of the House after 1976 (New Statesman, 31.10.80, p. 5). Perhaps one day they will let us know how they voted.

The Split

Immediately following the Special Conference in January 1981, which set up an electoral college to choose future party leaders giving the Trade Unions 40% of the votes, the PLP 30% and local parties 30%, 'the Three' now joined by Roy Jenkins who had finished his term as European

Commissioner in Brussels, formed the Council for Social Democracy (Guardian, 17.1.81, p. 1) and issued a short policy statement in line with the Open Letter. The next month Shirley Williams resigned from the Party's NEC. Owen and Rodgers had already refused to serve in Foot's shadow cabinet and on the 26th March the new party, the Social Democratic Party (SDP) was launched. In her letter of resignation, Shirley Williams confirmed that it was the question of reselection and the autonomy of MPs which was the immediate cause of her departure:

> The party that is now emerging is not the demo-
> cratic socialist party I joined, but a party intent on
> controlling those of its members who are elected to
> public office by the people of Britain. I believe
> that to be incompatible with the accountability of
> MPs and councillors to their electorate which lies
> at the heart of parliamentary democracy (Times,
> 10.2.81, p. 1)

I do not believe the question of the use of the block vote of the trade unions was of particular concern in itself, although its use in reducing the power of the parliamentary party certainly was. Atlee and Gaitskell had used the block vote to resist the Bevanites in the 1950s. William Rodgers, himself, had organised the block vote to reverse the decision on unilateralism in the early 1960s (Guardian Weekly, 8.3.81, p. 5), and Shirley Williams had been elected for the past 10 years by the trade unions to the NEC as a women's representative, in preference to contesting the constituency section, elected by individual members only, and risking defeat (Times, 12.2.81, p. 2). The timing of the decision to leave (following the Special Conference) was somewhat opportunistic, the decision of prin-ciple having been decided at the October Conference. Certainly the unpopularity of the trade unions with the public at large got the Social Democrats off to a good start. Part of the new party's programme was to form an electoral pact with the Liberals and, despite the fact that opinion polls in December 1980 showed a Foot-led Labour Party 12 points ahead of the Conservatives, almost all subsequent polls in 1981 suggested a Liberal-SDP alliance would outvote the other parties at any election held since then, although individually the parties would not do so well.

The Underlying Causes

However, while "the Three" were breaking with the Labour Party, other forces had been working to bring the split about from without. The most notable of these had been Roy Jenkins, David Marquand, who had quit parliament to join Jenkins in Brussels and who was now Professor of History and Politics at Salford University, and the Guardian Journalist, Peter Jenkins. Freed from the constraints of party life, these three were able to state more openly the underlying rather than the immediate reasons for the split. Subsequent writings and statements by those who quit Labour in 1981 have confirmed that the underlying reasons were often not stated in the debate leading to the split. Marquand now a member of the SDP's 12 man steering committee, called for a split immediately after the 1979 election in Encounter. Marquand's case was that the old Croslandite assumption that the purpose of social democracy was to increase the social wage as rapidly as possible, on which welfare-state social democrats of all parties used to act in practice, had collapsed (Marquand, 1979, p. 11). As a result he argued the old bureaucratic centralist programme was no longer valid and had to be abandoned but to do so would mean alienating not only the left, but also the old right of the party, particularly the trade unions (ibid, p. 18). The socialist and social democratic positions were now irreconcilable:

> The private sector is now so weak that a few more steps in a socialist direction might take it over the frontier. In these circumstances, the only possible strategy for a consistent social democrat who accepts the mixed economy as an end in itself...is to strengthen the private sector, to increase the share of national income going to profits and to tie Britain more firmly to the capitalist world. The logical strategy for a socialist must be to do the opposite (ibid, p. 17)

While welfare state socialism was to be abandoned, there was to be welfare for capitalism. As for social welfare, the answer was new forms of self-help (ibid, p. 11). As to the dilemma of the social democrats still in the party it was clear:

> What is needed now is to abandon both socialism and the kind of social democracy we have known since the war...So far, however, the social democrats have been careful not to upset the old right. Their chief aim has been to prevent the party from falling into the hands of the left (ibid, p. 18).

In the BBC Dimbleby Lecture in November 1979, Roy Jenkins announced he would return to politics after his sojourn in Brussells and called for a new centre party. He argued that the left could only be defeated by making the Labour Party more of a trade union party. Clearly, this was incompatible with his economic programme which was to place more emphasis on market forces and the free market economy (Jenkins, 1979, p. 20).

Marquand in The Spectator on the eve of the 1980 Conference returned to the same theme. He argued that the Labour right had lost the battle for ideas because it could not afford to alienate the unions, on whom it depended because it lacked troops in the constituency parties. Social democrats needed an economic policy but it was "simply not possible to devise a workable non-Marxist policy which did not entail conflict with the unions". In the circumstances, there was no alternative to a split:

It may not be possible for the social democratic
right to find a way out of this vicious circle outside
the Labour Party. It cannot conceivably do so
while its members depend for their political lives
on union votes; and so long as they remain inside
the Labour Party, they have no alternative but to
depend on union votes...indeed, if they win, they
will be tied to the unions even more firmly than
before. That, not an imaginary Bennite takeover,
provides the real case for a social democratic
breakout from the Labour Party (Marquand, 1980,
p. 11).

In an interview with The Advertiser, Shirley Williams later confirmed
the importance of the break with the trade unions:

We must end parties based on class. We may look
like intellectuals or any other dam thing, but the
fact that we are going to have a party which is not
affiliated to interest groups, whether middle class
and business, or so called blue-collar and union, is
in itself terribly important (25.3.81, p. 5)

In his book, Face the Future, David Owen seems to suggest, quite
wrongly, that Social Democrats in Europe have broken with the unions
(Owen, 1981, pp. 67-69) although the relationship is slightly different. He
also criticised Crosland as a bureaucratic centraliser and went on to advocate greater freedom for market forces and a reduction in the social limits
on its operations:

Advocates of the mixed economy must be prepared
to question the extent to which it is desirable to
mix the objectives of the public and private sector
- the extent to which inducing a sense of social
responsibility in the private sector is compatible
with the economic dynamic that should come from
the private entrepreneur...It is a serious criticism
that socialists who advocate a mixed economy must
face up to; that they risk emasculating the private
sector, by constraining its dynamic force, so limit-
ing its scope for initiative that its strengths and
economic contribution are sapped. The charge has
substance (Owen, 1981, pp. 44-45).

The underlying political causes of the split therefore become
clearer. It is not that the Labour Party is moving away from social democracy, rather a large part of the party is too attached to it. And as the
'Social Democrats' themselves have moved away from the social democratic consensus, they were forced to break with one of the institutions on
which both social democracy and even Keynesian economic programmes,
like "the New Deal" or "the Great Society", were built, the trade unions.
Finding that neo-Keynesian demand management alone no longer works and
not being prepared for a more radical programme of government intervention they are forced to fall back on market forces, even though as

Marquand admits the private sector will need propping up. As the economy heads into deeper recession they are moving in the opposite direction from that to which all the evidence of the post-depression decades points; a recession calls for more government intervention in the economy and not less. And that is what makes the break with the unions absolutely necessary for it is unlikely the unions could ever be won to that position. How little the move to the left in terms of policy played in the split is perhaps best emphasised by the fact that neither Owen nor Williams in full length books devote any space whatsoever to a critique of the Benn-Holland analysis and programme, although Owen does spend some time in a contradictory discussion of the Cambridge Economic Policy Group's proposals for import controls (Owen, 1981, pp. 131-132).

7.

THE POLITICAL ECONOMY OF CRISIS: POLICY OPTIONS IN THE 80s

Social Democrats in Search of a Policy

With little faith in Keynesian remedies maintaining the economy at a high level of activity and having abandoned their commitment to increasing the social wage and the welfare state, which is clearly the logical consequence of their disavowal of Croslandism and also their record in office, it is difficult to see what is left of social democracy in the accepted sense. This is clearly where the 'reborn' social democrats' problems begin for they have to put forward alternative policies and despite books from David Owen and Shirley Williams (Owen, 1981; Williams, 1981) and numerous articles and speeches, including a by-election campaign, there is very little that suggests even the beginnings of an alternative programme. This is not just a personal opinion, it is shared by most commentators. The attitude of the Director General of the Institute of Directors, Mr. Walter Goldsmith, is not untypical:

> The Social Democrats appear to have a public
> relations campaign, but absolutely no product to
> promote (Times, 27.3.81, p. 2).

Neither Owen's nor Williams' books have produced favourable reviews despite the strong support for the SDP in the media (New Society, 16.4.81, pp. 109-110; Economist, 31.1.81, pp. 81-82). The other problem is that the scale of the British economic disaster has also accelerated since Mrs. Thatcher came to office. Unemployment now stands at little short of 3 million, 12% of the workforce on official figures, which tend to underestimate by excluding many married women and others not entitled to benefit. Industrial production has fallen by more than 15% since 1979 and is still falling, considerably more than in the depression of 1929-31 (11%) (Times, 24.1.81, p. 12; 19.8.81, p. 1; Guardian Weekly, 11.1.81, p. 4). Investment is low, inflation is still higher than in 1979, and government expectations are that unemployment will move well over 3 million next year (Economist, 14.3.81, p. 30).

During the Warrington by-election, Roy Jenkins when questioned about economic recovery had this to say:

> The economy needs some stimulus, but it must be
> done in such a way as to produce the maximum
> impact on jobs for the minimum increase in public
> expenditure...And we need an end to the sterile
> frontier war beween public and private sectors to
> restore confidence to industry.

If you rule out much in the way of government expenditure, it seems there are three alternatives open; import controls, devaluation and an incomes policy harsh enough to reduce wages. Presumably for the SDP the first is ruled out because of EEC membership, and Britain's major trade deficit in manufactures is with the EEC (Owen, 1981, p. 124). Therefore we have devaluation and a strong incomes policy. Cambridge Econometrics have estimated that a 35% devaluation could create one million extra jobs and improve the balance of trade by 4 billion pounds annually. However, inflation would rise by another 10%, to well over 20% p.a., and living standards would fall by 4% (Kellner, New Stateman, 10.7.81, p. 5), and still leave unemployment at over 2 million. That leaves incomes policy, which is always to the fore of SDP propaganda. The trouble with effective incomes policies is that they require the sort of institutions to which the SDP claim to be opposed. Incomes policies are most effective in those countries which have strong corporatist institutions, in effect strong centralised trade unions and employer organisations which are able to negotiate at a national level and ensure their members comply: Austria, Scandinavia and West Germany (Bradley, 1981, p. 10). But so much of SDP thinking is opposed to corporatism and bureaucratic centralism that one must wonder which view will prevail (Owen, 1981, pp. 3-5; Williams, 1981, p. 180; Marquand, 1979, p. 9). Japan is also another corporatist society. One of the problems any government proposing an incomes policy in Britain will face is that British trade unions are not corporatist enough. Shop stewards and shop floor organisation are strong enough to thwart agreements made at the centre as they have often proved in the past (Owen, 1981, p. 47; Peter Jenkins, Guardian Weekly, 4.2.79, p. 3). Another problem with incomes policies is that in the past they have produced industrial and political strife as soon as it has become clear the aim is to keep wages down and reduce labour's share of GNP.

Shirley Williams has made the suggestion that small business, being more labour intensive, could make up for job losses in the giant capital intensive companies. Williams claims that the American experience has shown that this is a practical possibility (Williams, 1981, p. 96). She is quite right. Small business has generated perhaps as many as 11 million new jobs in the past decade. But what jobs? Contrary to Williams' assertion that these jobs were in high technology related fields with an emphasis on information services, the reality was rather different. The biggest increases were in employment in eating places like McDonalds, now a bigger employer than US Steel, health services, again mainly in the less skilled jobs and office services, essentially cleaning, caretaking and mailing. Retailing also showed a substantial increase (Will 1981, p. 4).

Another suggestion is to use the North Sea oil royalties for investment in industry (Open Letter, p. 11). This is also the policy of the Liberal Party, the TUC and the Labour left. With North Sea oil royalties rising rapidly, although they will probably peak by the mid-80s, this would appear to be a means of restructuring and modernising British industry. How it would square with a greater role for market forces is another matter but irrelevant. The truth is these funds are not available. They are being used to finance the recession. Despite their election commitment to reducing government expenditure, every item of government outlays except health and education, has risen since 1979 as a result of the recession and real public expenditure is now taking a full three points more of GNP than in 1979 (Davies and Piachaud, 1981, p. 16). North Sea oil royalties can only be used for investment if they are accompanied by swingeing tax increases to make up the shortfall, and which by reducing demand, would deepen the recession even further.

Against the Trend of Market Forces

The problem is that it is market forces and successive governments, Callaghan's and Thatcher's, committed to bowing to market forces, which are tending to marginalise Britain as a centre of industrial production. Multinational companies operating on an international basis, rather than on the basis of the national economy, now account for 66% of industrial production in Britain (S.J. Prais cited Benn, 1979, p. 50). Massive expansion in Britain in order to compete with themselves in Europe and the USA is unlikely and illogical so the question is therefore how to regenerate the national economy. Commenting on a programme advanced by the Liberal Party and almost identical to that put forward by the SDP, The Guardian called for reform of the financial institutions. Pointing out how little the Banks invested or loaned to industry and the comparatively unfavourable terms offered as opposed to Britain's competitors, it struck at the crux of the problem (Guardian, 13.1.81, p. 4; p. 10). There is no shortage of capital in Britain, the savings ratio is high, too high in fact, and Britain is still investing more overseas than West Germany and Japan combined (London CSE Group, 1979, p. 81; Guardian, 22.1.82, p. 18), the problem is the lack of profitable opportunities in industry. So the financial institutions invest overseas, buy government bonds at high rates of interest and generally speculate in paper, all of which produce higher money returns. The strength of Benn's position is that he recognises this and seeks to do something about it. The weakness of his position is that his programme is not supported by any new constituency which can implement it so that it can only be brought in based on the agreement of industry and finance, neither of which shows any signs of being prepared to do so. Benn's policy of itself cannot resolve the question of the supply and quality of management and it would have to rely on the existing civil service and business community. It is that which makes his programme corporatist rather than any intent. Indeed in his public utterances he is even more anti-corporatist than the SDP (Benn 1979, p. 140; p. 145-6; p. 111; Guardian Weekly, 30.9.79, p. 5). The other problem for Benn is that his programme is for the long term regeneration of British Industry and he has no short term programme distinguishable from the rest of the Labour Party. However, the difficulties do not eliminate Labour's need for a programme which seeks to revive the national economy. In The General Theory Keynes recognised that government influence on banking policy and the rate of interest (and he did not envisage interest rates reaching the present absurd levels) would be insufficient "to determine an optimum rate of investment". He therefore foresaw that "a somewhat comprehensive socialisation of investment will prove the only means of securing an approximation to full employment" (Keynes, 1973, pp. 378-379). More recently the American economist, Lester C. Thurow in The Zero-Sum Society returned to the same theme. Discussing the problem of low growth economies, and the OECD now estimates it will take a 3% growth rate merely to maintain present levels of employment (Australian, 7.8.81, p. 13), he rejected central economic planning but advocated a National Corporate Investment Committee and a National Investment Bank to direct investment flows and to ensure potential growth sectors were not short of funds (Thurow, 1980, p. 96; p. 191). In a recent submission to an ALP Seminar on "The Socialist Objective", the Adelaide University Keynesian, Geoff Harcourt went even further arguing not only for the direction of investment, but also for the nationalisation of major private firms and for the need for the state sector to generate a surplus to "fulfill its redistributive goal" (Howe, 1981, p. 2). If there is to be the regeneration of national economies, and it is difficult to see how anything aproaching full employment and stable living standards can be obtained and maintained if they are not, then to a large extent they will have to be rebuilt against the trend of market forces on a world scale.

No Policy as a Policy?

The dilemma for the SDP, and for the Labour Party for that matter, is that there are no moderate policies which go anywhere towards resolving the British economic crisis. There are no sensible policies to which everyone can agree and which do not involve someone, or some large section to be more exact, getting hurt. The recession has gone too far for that. Whether you choose to lower living standards by devaluation, incomes policy, import controls or inflation, or to enforce planning agreements on industry or direction of funds on finance you are embarked on confrontation not consensus politics in anything but the short term. Even reducing the influence of rentier interests, the necessity for which Keynes recognised in the 1930s, has become a formidable task. Most of us, with our pension schemes and insurance policies, are rentiers in part now. As Thurow rightly proclaims:

> As we head into the 1980s, it is well to remember
> that there is really only one important question in
> political economy. If elected, whose income do you
> and your party plan to cut in the process of solving
> the economic problems facing us? (Thurow, 1980,
> p. 214).

This is almost certainly what is behind the reluctance of the new social democrats to commit themselves to definite policies. In fact having no definite policy could almost be said to be the policy of the SDP. Questioned in Southampton on the day of the party's launching as to their policy, David Owen replied "Look love, if you want a manifesto, go and join one of the other parties" (Times, 27.3.81, p. 2). Roy Jenkins has often spoken of the disease of "manifestoism" and Peter Jenkins in the Guardian has gone as far as to argue that policies are just what political parties do not need and that the result of having them can only be to disappoint their supporters when they discover they cannot be carried out (New Statesman, 27.3.81, p. 2). It is therefore fairly pertinent to ask whether in seeking to offer a soft option between Thatcher and unrestrained financial market forces and Benn and 'corporatism', the SDP are putting forward any more than an empty shell for those who do not wish to make the hard choice to vote for. Are they offering no more than sit tight and hope things work out for the best? A fairly frightening retort to such wishful thinking has recently come from Francis Cripps in the Cambridge Journal of Economics who suggests that if the present process of deindustrialisation continues, with further closures and continuing import penetration, the UK might not be able to support much more than half the present population of 55 million in conditions of full employment and reasonable living standards once North Sea Oil has run out (C.J.E., 5, 1981, p. 99). Action to restructure and regenerate the economy cannot be avoided. That action will almost certainly require a higher level of government intervention than before, quite literally to counter market forces. Economic policy is clearly the "achilles heel" of the social democrats.

As if almost to confirm the difficulties of social democracy geared to market forces, the West German crisis is now upon us. Faced with a growing trade deficit, 6.2 billion pounds in the current year, rising government expenditure, the declining value of the Deutshe Mark and pressure on interest rates, the West German Government recently announced an unprecedented 4 billion pound cut in public expenditure, more than half of which was to be borne by the social welfare programme. These measures were taken at a time of rising unemployment, more than 1.2 million are out of work, falling investment and negative economic growth since mid-1980 (Times, 31.7.81, p. 1). Unemployment may seem low by UK standards but conceals the fact that West Germany alone of leading Western Countries has seen a fall in the workforce since 1973, reflecting the fact that many immigrants have been forced to go home (Will, 1981, p. 4).

But Has Labour A Policy?

The Labour Party on the other hand has been only too willing to commit itself to clear policies. The result however is that it is beginning to look as "bankrupt" as the SDP. Playing down the Benn-Holland programme of restructuring the public sector to generate more investment and more competition, basically because the parliamentary leadership neither supports it nor believes it feasible, the present emphasis is on a massive programme of public investment of the conventional type. By far the most ambitious public spending plan put forward is by the TUC. Its recent document, Plan for Growth, calls for public investment of 24 billion pounds over the next five years. By its own admission even this massive programme would only create, directly and indirectly, 500,000 "real jobs" (Keegan, 1981, p. 16; Kellner, New Statesman, 3.7.81, p. 5). However, as a number of commentators quickly pointed out, this would do no more than offset the likely rise in unemployment over the next few years. It would also by increasing demand suck in imports creating a balance of payments problem unless accompanied by import controls and if accompanied by such controls would be inflationary. This is not because increased government spending necessarily equals inflation. It probably doesn't in conditions of slack demand (or if countered by tax increases), but because the trade unions would seek to make up for lost ground and cause cost-push inflationary price rises. If wages were restrained, the extra demand would almost certainly produce a speculative boom in real estate, commodities and paper with inflationary implications for the whole economy as in 1972-73. The scale of the problem is now beyond traditional demand management responses alone. Other Labour promises such as lower direct and indirect taxes and lower interest rates although patently necessary for any long term recovery, would have little short term effect on employment. Labour is equally faced with the problem of whose living standards are to fall and how to achieve it by consent. It is now near certain that only structural change can revive Britain's fortunes and the only two structural thinkers around are Thatcher and Benn. With the evidence increasing all the time that Thatcher's market forces are not going to work, it cannot be long before the case for Benn's programme, whether to be implemented by Benn or by an acceptable "moderate", becomes politically overwhelming, which nonetheless will not guarantee its success.

8.
THE FUTURE OF LABOUR AND THE SOCIAL DEMOCRATS

The Conservative Slide Continues

Fortunately for both the SDP and the Labour Party their absence of policy is somewhat overshadowed by the disasters of the Thatcher Government. All the long term indicators now suggest that the economy will still be in recession and still on the way down by the next election in 1984 (Keegan, 1981, p. 16). The possibility that Thatcher and her policies will be ditched in an attempt to recapture the centre ground before the next election, are receding. On what policies would a U-turn be based? But more importantly because of the enormous bankbench support enjoyed by Thatcher. While there is opposition in the Tory establishment (the Party President, Lord Thornecroft's attack on Thatcher's policies in September 1981, is an indication of this), backbench opinion is demanding a purge of cabinet "wets" and a totally Thatcherite cabinet (Australian, 2.9.81, p. 5; Times, 3.8.81, p. 1).

The Division of Labour

Labour's most pressing problem is to resolve its internal differences and to reach a workable compromise. There is as yet no sign that the Parliamentary Party is prepared to make any concessions in the direction of its greater accountability to the party at large or to accepting Conference decisions in terms of the policies it pursues in Parliament. Despite overwhelming Conference votes, neither the alternative economic strategy, nor unilateralism, nor opposition to American bases are in any way part of the PLP policy at the present time. Having won all the debates but being met by a brick wall the constituency activists are becoming increasingly resentful of the PLP and all the evidence suggests an increasingly bitter feeling within the Party. It is not only the intransigence of the PLP but also the continuous misrepresentation of the left's case by the media which serve to keep the Party in a state of crisis (New Statesman, 23.1.81, p. 2). An article by The Advertiser's London Correspondent, Graham Clark recently comparing Benn with Stalin, gave Australians a taste of the campaign of denigration (Advertiser, 5.9.81, p. 5). The feeling that argument and democratic decision making can make no progress in the party is leading to a situation wherein organisational manoeuvre is replacing political debate. Another problem the party will have to resolve is the question of the trade union block vote in its decision making. The undemocratic nature of trade union decision making is a major cause for concern, leaving a few powerful general secretaries, often unelected, with enormous power (Guardian Weekly, 21.6.81, p. 10). The block vote has normally favoured the right it should be noted (Times, 2.2.81, p. 17).

As if to emphasise the gap between the PLP and the rest of the party, the 1981 Conference agenda contained not a single resolution to reverse or alter the January vote to establish an electoral college to elect future leaders, despite a 144 to 24 votes by the PLP to assert their right to at least the largest share in future elections (Times, 5.3.81, p. 2; 20.7.81 p. 1). Clearly, the current differences between the PLP and the party membership at large cannot continue without doing severe damage to the party, particularly if the resolution of these differences increasingly takes an organisational form. Because of its record of governmental failure, it is looking increasingly as if it is the PLP which will finally have to bend, particularly with reselection a weapon in the hands of the party activists.

A lot of media attention has been given to alleged takeovers of local parties by "extremists" from Marxist organisations like "Militant". The evidence for this it has to be said is scant although it makes good copy for the party's detractors in the media. Recently a right-wing MP, John Sever, was deselected in the Birmingham Constituency of Ladywood. The press condemned his ousting as a "Militant takeover". The reality was different. A Militant candidate stood and gained 4 votes. The winner was a supporter of Tribune, University Lecturer Albert Bore. Sever's difficulties seem to have begun when he called for the use of troops to break strikes in the public sector in 1979 (New Statesman, 29.5.81, pp. 4-5). If there is a takeover of local parties it is that a well-educated middle class activist is replacing the traditional working class Labour Party Member. A recent survey (Whiteley 1981) found that the new activists were very independent-minded, excessively concerned with democratic procedures and parochial questions, increasingly middle class or at least white-collar, and increasingly employed in the public sector. They were also at least as well-educated as MPs and therefore were able to take them to task when the need or opportunity arose (ibid, pp. 160-170).

However, it should not be thought that the present mood of intolerance is all one way traffic as an articulate activist membership attacks an incompetent parliamentary leadership. There are increasingly strident attacks by "the moderates" on the left. Even The Economist was moved to comment on the attacks on the 'leftist' leader of the Greater London Council, Ken Livingstone by the party leaders. Livingstone attacked police behaviour before and during the last summer's urban disturbances and supported the Irish hunger strikers. He is also proposing a Bennite programme of public enterprise to revive London's economy and a London Enterprise Board to assist private enterprise to set up in the capital with loans and premises. The "latest hate-figure of the right wing press and the Parliamentary Party" was The Economist's description of Livingstone (15.8.81, pp. 21-23). Nor does the right wing's refusal to discuss the economic and political issues at stake openly help the cause of tolerance. Misrepresentation is the name of the game as they claim they have been trying to save the party from extremism. The reality of the Benn-Holland programme as I have argued throughout, is that it is no more than a radical Keynesian programme and may well be, despite its problems, the softest option available.

Electoral Prospect

As for the party's internal problems effect on the electorate, Labour's lead throughout 1981 was barely enough to win the next election in a contest with the Conservatives never mind with the intervention of the Social Democrats (Kellner, New Statesman, 15.5.81, p. 5).

Internal dispute is not necessarily a cause of unpopularity. Labour enjoyed a large lead in the polls in 1952-53 during the Bevanite rows and between 1961 and 1964 when the debate over unilateralism was at its height. On the other hand, Labour support collapsed in 1977 in a quiet period after the government accepted the IMF terms without a single resignation (B. Page New Statesman, 28.9.79, p. 449). However, the present bickering, as opposed to a serious debate, is hardly conducive to electoral popularity.

Despite the Social Democrats' estimation that the centre ground is where the electorate is to be found, the evidence is rather to the contrary and represents a major threat to Labour. The social geography of Britain is becoming more polarised with both Labour and Conservatives piling up their votes in safe seats, while the number of marginal constituencies, susceptible to change on a swing of 5% or less, continues to decline. In the 1950s and 1960s, there were approximately 200 marginals, now there are little more than 100. To win in 1984, Labour needs to win another 64 seats but there are only 63 Conservative marginals. Labour needs a swing of 7%, the largest at any election since the war, to win the next election (New Statesman, 2.1.81, p. 5).

This is where the SDP challenge comes in. For although the SDP set itself up as an alternative to Labour, the present indications are that it is likely to do more electoral damage to and take more votes from the Conservatives than from Labour. This is certainly the evidence of their two earliest major tests, the Warrington by-election and the County Council elections in Lincoln where there was an existing social democratic organisation around Dick Taverne. In the first, Labour held the seat with a sharply reduced majority while the Conservative candidate was annihilated. In the latter SDP intervention turned a marginal Conservative Council into a safe Labour one (Times, 19.7.81, pp. 1-2; Kellner, New Statesman, 15.3.81, p. 5). Even the most recent opinion polls continue to show this trend which has moved ex-Thatcher Minister, Norman St. John-Stevas to describe the SDP-Liberal Alliance as the gravest challenge yet to the Conservative Party (Times, 21.8.81, p. 2). Thus having split from Labour in order to deny them office, the SDP is faced with the possibility of letting Labour gain office in 1984 with little more than 30% of the vote, unless they can themselves maintain their present opinion poll levels of support. Past precedent suggests otherwise. Mid-term has generally been the high point of third party support as the Liberals well know. In 1962, Liberal Eric Lubbock turned a Tory majority of 14,760 into a Liberal victory by 7855, and in 1973 at Chester-le-Street, the Liberals contesting the seat for the first time gained 18,808 votes (38.6%) against Labour. Both these by-election triumphs dwarf Roy Jenkins' effort at Warrington in gaining 42% of the vote and reducing the Labour vote by 5026. Warrington was not the by-election sensation of the century as the press would tell us. He had a solid Liberal base to build on, 18% in 1974 and benefited from being a national figure against two mediocre candidates, a trade union official and a Thatcherite bus driver, got more media coverage and engaged in 'red scare' tactics against the Labour candidate. The other difficulty posed for the SDP is that the first past the post system makes it difficult to do moderately well at general elections. The SDP-Liberal Alliance at first set themselves the task of gaining the balance of power in the next Parliament. This is in fact the hardest thing to do as parties tend to do very well in terms of seats gained or very badly relative to their vote, as the Liberals have often found. Because their vote is more concentrated than either the Conservatives or the Liberals, or the SDP-Liberal Alliance if the opinion polls are correct, a three-way split favours Labour. On the other hand, were the Conservative vote to fall below 30% the result would be devastating, a mere handfall of seats. The SDP may therefore produce for themselves the worst of all worlds by making Labour's accession to government easier not more difficult: the complete reverse of the intention behind the split (Kellner, <u>New Statesman</u>, 10.4.81, p. 5; <u>Tribune</u>, 24.7.81, p. 1; p. 3).

Other sobering thoughts for the SDP must concern their alliance with the Liberals. While the alliance seems to be going smoothly at national level, this is not the case at the grass roots. Liberal Associations are not happy to, nor seem prepared to cede winnable seats to SDP candidates and both parties are mainly interested in middle class suburban type seats, rather than Labour's inner city strongholds. The refusal of a Liberal candidate to stand down in favour of Shirley Williams for the Croydon by-election despite David Steel's pleading is evidence enough of the friction as was the statement by the Association of Liberal Councillors telling local parties not to cede any Liberal held council seats to the SDP (<u>Times</u>, 18.7.81, p. 1; 21.7.81, p. 1; 18.8.81, p. 1). From the SDP side, Mike Thomas MP complained that Liberals were hogging all the best seats because they had candidates already in position. His fear was that an SDP-Liberal victory would produce a majority of Liberal MPs (<u>Times</u>, 24.7.81, p. 1).

Another interesting question concerns what will happen in an elitist organisation like the SDP with its postal consultations with the membership when serious differences of opinion arise in the party as they are sure to do. We have already seen a public slanging match between Shirley Williams and Dick Taverne over the latter's idea of decentralising the education system along the American pattern (Kellner, <u>New Statesman</u>, 5.2.81, p. 5). Shirley Williams' view of the absurdity of measuring economic efficiency only in terms of the productivity of labour in a world long on people and short on energy, raw materials and land (Williams 1981, p. 100) would seem to fly in the face of Jenkins, Marquand, Horam and Owen's market forces and therefore to be a potential source of acrimony. Plebicitary parties like plebicitary governments are not geared towards the resolution of differences by debate and compromise. That requires normal party life.

The birth of the SDP therefore does not signal the end of Labour as a governing party nor does it signal the rebirth of social democracy in Britain. What it probably means is that a new centre-right party has taken up that part of the middle ground currently vacated by the Conservative Party and it is the viability of the latter at least in the medium term that looks in danger.

POSTSCRIPT

As we go to press, the Thatcher government is currently enjoying a level of electoral popularity that would have seemed impossible a few months ago, as a result of the "Falklands factor". On a wave of patriotism, some might even say "jingoism", resulting from the military "adventure" in the South Atlantic, the Conservatives have won two parliamentary by-elections and maintained their position in local government elections held since the crisis broke in the first week of April 1982. However, it is difficult to believe that this new found support will last far beyond the realisation of the costs of "victory" and the political quagmire "victory" will create. A permanent garrison of perhaps 4,000 troops will have to be stationed in the Falklands for the forseeable future, backed by a naval force including a nuclear submarine and at least a squadron of harrier jets. New communications, air and sea links will have to be established to replace the old ones with Argentina probably directly with Britain via Ascension Island. The garrison itself and British supply lines may well continue to be, at least, harassed by Argentina for some time. Indeed, Argentina has already made it clear such will be the case and having committed Britain to such a massive response, it will be politically very difficult for the government to enter into serious negotiations with Argentina in the immediate future, even assuming the latter would be willing. Prediction is always difficult in politics as the Falklands crisis has demonstrated but I suspect we will be back to a political situation dominated by the economy and its problems by the end of the year. However, by then the costs of the Falklands will have been added to the already seemingly intractable economic crisis. It would be foolish, however, not to admit that the "Falklands factor" has thrown a "wild card" into any speculation on the outcome of the next general election.

Prior to the Falklands crisis the Liberal/SDP Alliance had won three stunning by-election victories in safe Conservative seats to which it had added more than 100 victories in local by-elections. Roy Jenkins after his triumph in Hillhead had looked certain to lead the SDP in Parliament, despite Shirley Williams and David Owen's pretensions, and the Alliance at the next general election. However, following his poor parliamentary showing during the crisis, it is Jenkin's leadership qualities that look in question. Healey defeated Benn for the Labour deputy leadership at the October Conference by a whisker, and, following a period of bitter infighting, an agreed truce between right and left was arrived at, or rather was imposed by the Trade Union leaders at the Bishop Stortford meeting in January 1982. Labour's electoral showing, however, continues to be poor. It has been pushed into third place in each of the by-elections. The Conservatives for their part continue to preside over an economy showing no signs of halting its precipitous decline.

In the economy, the only sign of relief for the government is that the rate of increase in unemployment appears to have slowed down. The underlying monthly increase has averaged 20,000 this year as against 50,000 in the summer of 1981 and 100,000 in the second half of 1980. The March total was 2,992,000 dipping below 3 million as year-end school-leavers found jobs. This is approximately 12.5% of the workforce but this only includes people officially registered as actively looking for work and is clearly an under-estimate of the real total of unemployment (Times, 24.3.82, p. 1). January manufacturing output was the lowest since 1967, 19% down since Mrs. Thatcher came to power. Overall industrial production fell by more than 1% in each of the three months to January 1982 despite record North Sea Oil production and is more than 15% below the 1979 figure, itself hardly a bumper year (Australian, 17.2.82; Australian Financial Review, 22.3.82 p. 7). The 1982/83 budget, although not as severe as in previous years, gave little away and most commentors agree that the man, or woman, on average wages or below will be worse off as increases in indirect taxes more than eat up the savings from the index-ation of basic tax allowances. Mrs. Thatcher and her ministers continue to predict that the recession has bottomed and that recovery is in sight. However, their views are in marked contrast to the evidence and are flatly contradicted by the Confederation of British Industry. The CBI sees no sign of recovery and its members expect to see another quarter million unemployed by mid-year if the government persists with its overall economic policy. 93% of CBI members continue to work below capacity (Times, 3.2.82, p. 1). Productivity in industry has risen some 8% in the last two years but there is considerable doubt as to whether this represents long term improvement or is merely normal phenomena in a recession, due to redundancies, which will not last once production picks up and it also conceals the fact that productivity fell 6% in 1979-80. The evidence of past economic downturns, 1972-74 and 1975-77 suggests the latter.(Kellner, New Statesman, 13.11.81, pp. 9-10).

To those unfamiliar with the first past the post electoral system, the spectacular Alliance victories in Croydon North-West, Crosby and Hillhead might have seemed to indicate that the political mould really had been broken and that the Alliance would be odds-on to win the next general election with a clear majority. To the initiated it would have been clear that such was not the case. The evidence of the opinion polls and the last "normal" by-election, Hillhead, if taken on a seat by seat basis, suggested that despite the Alliance having more votes than either of the other two parties, it was Labour which would have emerged as the largest party, if short of an overall majority, from a general election, and that despite its having not only less votes than the Alliance but less than the Conservatives as well. Such are the vagaries of the British electoral system. In a three way contest, with votes split fairly evenly, the system favours Labour because its vote is heavily concentrated in its own seats. Unlike the other two parties, Labour can win outright with about 30% of the vote (Times, 27.2.82, p. 2; Kellner, New Statesman, 30.10.81, p. 6). The next election is, however, still wide open. The speculation must therefore be as to whether the Conservatives would be tempted to enter a coalition with the Alliance to keep Labour out. The problem for the Conservatives would be that they might have to concede proportional representation, to which the Alliance is committed but to which they are, like Labour, decidedly hostile as it could make coalition government a permanent feature of British political life and virtually rule out either of the old parties forming a government in its own right again.

There are a number of other question marks concerning the Alliance. Of the first four by-elections, the SDP put up a big-name national figure in three. In these elections they have picked up a fairly uniform 80% plus of the votes lost by the Labour and Conservative candidates (Jenkins-Warrington 81%; Williams-Crosby 86%; Jenkins-Hillhead 84%). However, at Croydon North-West a non-national figure, Bill Pitt, although winning the seat could only gather 57% of the votes lost by his rivals since 1979, the rest abstaining. This is not because Pitt was a Liberal. The Liberal vote is holding up extremely well and in local elections the Liberals are doing, if anything, better than the SDP (Kellner, New Statesman, 11.1.82, p. 4; Ibid, 14.5.82, p. 4). The indications would seem to be that a national figure is capable of attracting more of the votes of those dissatisfied with the older parties than a less well known local figure. This is hardly surprising but the Alliance may find subsequent by-elections, now that all the well known personalities have seats, harder to win with ordinary run of the mill candidates. Only time will tell on that one but too much should not be read into the Beaconsfield and Merton and Morden by-elections for the longer term future of the SDP. There were too many abnormal factors.

Another doubt concerns the "clean" image of the SDP. The original adherents presented without doubt a fairly principled picture but sub-sequent defectors to it have rather tarnished that image. Some of these have quit for entirely opportunistic reasons, such as losing their seats through boundary redistribution, while others who have found their way into the party may not have been entirely welcome. Nowhere is this clearer than with the situation in Islington. One of the Islington MPs, O'Halloran quit to join the SDP when faced with the possibility of deselection. Within months he was followed by a majority of the local Labour Councillors and the SDP gained control of its first council. O'Halloran was selected as Labour candidate for Islington North, a very safe seat, in 1969 in dubious circumstances. 21 of 54 delegates to the meeting were admitted barely in time to qualify to vote. Of the 21, at least nine subsequently proved to be non-resident and in some cases proved impossible to trace at all. One 'real' delegate, who was on holiday, returned to find his vote had been cast on his behalf by persons unknown. The SDP Councillors were led by one William Bayliss, who for many years ran the Council and the local Labour Party as a "rotten borough". These are hardly the representatives to change the mould of British politics and their acceptance into the SDP raises serious questions as to what sort of party is likely to emerge. The latest news is that Bayliss is already in trouble with his local SDP branch. This is not an isolated incident. There are quesion marks over many of the local defectors to the party. One of the attractions of the SDP, in these circumstances, is its claim that elected representatives are not answerable to the local party (New Statesman, 11.9.81, p. 4; Ibid, 11.12.81, pp. 4-5).

The problem of the distribution of parliamentary seats between Liberals and SDPers has still not been resolved. The deadline for agreement, 31 March 1982, has come and gone and there were still some 120 seats undecided, in many cases the most contentious. The problem of compatibility between the over-centralised SDP and the fairly decentralised Liberals continues. The crisis that broke in December when William Rodgers broke off negotiations because Steel would not, and indeed could not, overrule local Liberal Associations does not bode entirely well for the future (Australian, 2.4.81, p. 4). As if to confirm that the Alliance represents more of an electoral threat to the Conservatives than to Labour, all but a handful of the most contentious seats, contentious because they are the most winnable, are Conservative held (Guardian, 11.1.82, p. 10).

As for policy, in particular economic policy, the SDP remains silent. For a time Roy Jenkins appeared interested in Professor Layard's inflation tax, a special tax on inflationary price rises and thereby indirectly on inflationary wage settlements, as a form of price control but it has been dropped as quickly as it was taken up. The anti-trade union bias of the party became clearer when a majority of SDP MPs including its leaders supported Norman Tebbit's Bill to drastically reduce the immunities from civil damages that British trade unions have enjoyed for the last 60 years (Times, 9.2.82, p. 1). The SDP are rather caught in a cleft stick as regards policy. At the moment all the poll evidence suggests most people are voting for them in revulsion from the existing parties. Theirs is a negative vote. However, their new supporters are voting for them for mutually incompatible reasons. Some are voting SDP because they consider the Conservatives and Labour too radical. They want stability. Others are voting for them because they want change. They are voting against the incompetence of the government and opposition. The SDP cannot satisfy both groups (Times, 27.3.82, p. 8). Their reluctance to commit themselves to definite policies is therefore twofold. People can vote against policies they don't like e.g. too strong a support for the EEC. The other is more serious. The economic crisis is now so intractable that it is difficult to see which moderate middle of the road policies would have any chance of success and once proposed they would be exposed as totally inadequate from all parts of the political spectrum. At the moment the SDP, and the Alliance for that matter, are enjoying success without responsibility.

For the Labour Party the picture is fairly gloomy. To a large extent the party is being protected from its long-term electoral decline by the first past the post system. Despite its poor showing in recent by-elections it can still hope to be the largest party after the next election. However, the system does not protect it from the political as opposed to the electoral consequences of its decline. If Labour were to be elected with 30% or even less of the vote as majority party, as is quite possible on a three way split, it might well face a legitimacy crisis in office which would sharply circumscribe its ability to take radical measures in the face of the serious economic situation. Even if the electoral system does favour Labour, the necessity to increase its electoral support cannot be avoided. It is certainly unpopular to say so but the right-wing of the party must bear a much heavier responsibility for the present low esteem in which the party is held than the left. It is not possible for the right to publicly claim that the party is being taken over by "extremists and loonies", which is blatantly untrue as this analysis has argued throughout, and not expect to do themselves and the party enormous electoral damage. This sort of self abuse had reached such heights after the 1981 Conference that it would have been pertinent to ask leading members of the parliamentary party if they had entirely written off the next general election and considered the defeat of Benn and the "new left" more important than the defeat of Thatcher.

At the Conference, Healey retained the deputy leadership by less than one per cent. 83% of Constituency Parties voted for Benn in the first ballot and more than 90% in the second. Clear majorities of MPs and trade unions however voted for Healey. (Kogan, 1982, p. 146). In the elections to the NEC the left's majority was reduced to a wafer thin 15-14. However the majorities for most of the left policies on the economy and defence hardened. Despite Benn's strong showing in the deputy leadership contest he was denied a place in the shadow cabinet, the elections to which confirmed that the right was still firmly in control of the parliamentary party (Times, 20.11.81, p. 1). Reselection is beginning to have its effect on the composition of future Parliamentary Labour Parties. It is not so much that sitting Labour MPs are being replaced by more radical aspirants, although there have been a few displaced in this manner, but that retiring members are being replaced by new candidates well to their left in many cases (Kogan, 1982, p. 150). At the end of the year, the NEC refused to endorse a selected candidate, Peter Tatchell and announced an enquiry into the

Militant tendency. The decision not to endorse Tatchell was indefensible. He was not associated with any "extremist" group and his sole crime, except for being on the left of the party, was that he called for extra-parliamentary action to supplement parliamentary opposition to Thatcher's policies. As most of the Labour front bench were engaged in just such actions (i.e. leading demonstrations against unemployment) the charge had a hollow ring about it. In the furore that followed, the trade unions were forced to step in and impose a degree of order and a compromise. Unlike MPs, the trade unions cannot afford to write off the next election with 3 million unemployed. The compromise appears to be, for details were not disclosed, that the right will endorse duly selected candidates, take no action on the enquiry and accept Conference decisions on the economy and defence. For its part the left will not contest the leadership and will not seek further constitutional changes. How this will work out only time will tell but such a precarious balance will be hard to maintain and past precedent would not give much grounds for optimism. The general disarray and the poor performance of the Foot-Healey leadership during the Falklands crisis would seem to confirm this pessimistic perspective.

Some indication of the hollowness of the "extremist" takeover came out in the New Year when it emerged that there were seven Militant supporters endorsed as parliamentary candidates, out of a total of more than 600 candidates. As Militant has been practicing an entry tactic in the Labour Party for more than 20 years, and many of the local parties it has taken over were mere shells devoid of members as in Liverpool, it has to be said that the Militant takeover is an extremely gradualist affair. Militant is also by far the largest of the "extremist" groups operating in the party (Guardian, 25.1.82, p. 1; J. Callaghan, New Statesman, 26.2.82, pp. 609). The presence of Militant merely provides the right with a convenient whipping boy. The reality of the "new left" in the local parties is far from the extremist image portrayed by the media. Even support for the welfare state and local services is liable to have you branded as left wing in places like Islington.

One criticism of the original essay was that it had failed to point out the radicalising effect the struggle for party democracy was having on the activists. Certainly there has been a radicalising effect but it tends to rather prove the basic thesis of this essay. Despite being radicalised the "new left" has directed its growing militancy into constitutional channels quite unlike the effects radicalisation had on the generation of the 1960s, whose militancy took on extra-parliamentary and often revolutionary forms. The present radicalisation is reformist in a way the former never was.

One of the few encouraging things about Labour at the moment is that it seems to have dropped the "monetarist" thinking which served it so badly during its last period of government. However the version of the Alternative Economic Strategy which is now being heard from official sources is more a neo-Keynesian variant than the Holland/Benn radical Keynesian policy. It emphasises increasing demand, reducing interest rates, public works and some measures of import controls. It addresses itself only vaguely, if at all, to the long term problem of restructuring British industry, in particular manufacturing, the necessity for which is becoming more evident every day as decline, redundancies and closures continue (Times, 16.3.82, p. 3; Kellner, New Statesman, 5.2.82, p. 5). Unlike the other parties, this is a question which the Labour Party, with its trade union links and greater dependence on working class votes, cannot avoid. As international market forces continue to drive British industry to the wall the necessity, if not yet the electoral pressure, for a more interventionist state becomes more apparent by the hour. That is Labour's challenge, failure to grasp the nettle, could be its demise.

BIBLIOGRAPHY

Primary Sources:

Newspapers etc.:

The Australian

The Economist

The Guardian

The Guardian Weekly

Marxism Today

The New Statesman

Socialist Commentary (S.C. ceased publication December 1977)

The Times

Tribune (London)

Other Primary Sources:

Bealey, Frank (ed.), The Social & Political Thought of the British Labour
        Party, Weidenfeld & Nicholson, 1970.

Benn, Tony, Arguments for Socialism, London, Cape, 1979

Crosland, Anthony, The Future of Socialism, London, MacMillan, 1956
        The Future of Socialism, New York, MacMillan, 1957
        'The Future of the Left', Encounter, March, 1960
        The Conservative Enemy, London, Cape, 1962
        The British Economy in 1965, Nottingham, University Press,
        1965.
        Social Objectives for the 1970s, The Times, 25th September,
        1970
        Socialism Now and Other Essays, London, Cape, 1975(a)
        Social Democracy in Europe, London, Fabian Tract, 1975(b)
        'Equality in Hard Times', Socialist Commentary, October, 1976

Foot, Michael, 'Credo of the Labour Left', New Left Review, 49, 1968.

Hattersley, Roy, 'The True Crosland Creed', The Guardian, 15th January
        1981, p. 10
        'Why I Will Stay on and Fight', Sunday Times, 25th January 1981,
        p. 12

Holland, Stuart, The Socialist Challenge, London, Quartet, 1978

Horam, John, 'Social Democracy's Stand in the Market Place', The Guardian, 19th January 1981, p. 7
'Born Again Social Democrats', Spectator, 7th March 1981, p. 15.

Jenkins, Roy, 'The Dimbleby Lecture', Guardian Weekly, 2nd December 1979

Liberal Party, "10-point plan for Economic Recovery", The Guardian, 13th January 1981, p. 4.

Manifesto Group, 'What we must do', Socialist Commentary, December 1976

Marquand, David, 'Inquest on a Movement', Encounter, July 1979
'Why Labour cannot be saved', Spectator, 27th September 1980

Owen, David, Face the Future, London, Cape, 1981

Owen, David, Rodgers, William, and Williams Shirley, 'Open Letter to the Labour Party', The Guardian, 1st August 1980, p. 11

Rodgers William, 'Socialism Without Abundance', Socialist Commentary, July-August 1977

Social Democratic Party, Twelve Tasks for Social Democrats, The Times, 27th March 1981, p. 2

Williams, Shirley, Interview, Newsweek, 23rd February 1981
Interview, The Advertiser, 25th March 1981, p. 5
Politics is for People, London, Penguin, 1981

Wilson, Harold, The Relevance of British Socialism, London, Weidenfeld & Nicholson, 1964
Final Term: The Labour Government 1974-76, London, Weidenfeld & Nicholson, 1979

Secondary Sources:

I have used the regular columns of Peter Jenkins in the Guardian Weekly, Peter Kellner and Patrick Wintour in the New Statesman extensively. I have resorted to the following expedient when citing from these sources:

Peter Jenkins, G.W., ...
Peter Kellner, N.S., ...
Patrick Wintour, N.S., ...

Bacon, Robert and Eltis, Walter, Britain's Economic Problem: Too Few Producers, London, MacMillan, 1976

Balogh, Thomas, Labour and Inflation, London, Fabian Tract, 1970

Barratt-Brown, Michael, 'The Welfare State in Britain', Socialist Register 1971

Beckerman, Wilfred, (ed.) Labour's Economic Record: 1964-70, London, Duckworth, 1972
(ed.) Slow Growth in Britain: Causes and Consequences, Oxford, Clarendon, 1979

Bell, Daniel, 'Anthony Crosland and Socialism', Encounter, August 1977

Blackburn, Robin, 'The Heath Government: A New Course for British Capitalism', New Left Review, 70, 1971

Bosanquet, Nicholas 'Three Lessons from Labour's Economic Record', Socialist Commentary, July 1970

Bradley, Ian, 'Birth Pangs of the Party that was Nearly not born at all', The Times, 3/4th August 1981

Caves, Richard and Krause, Lawrence, Britain's Economic Performance, Washington, Brooking Institutue, 1980

Coates, David, The Labour Party and the Struggle for Socialism, London, Cambridge, 1975
Labour in Power?, London, Longman, 1980

Coutts, Ken et al, 'The Economic Consequences of Mrs. Thatcher', Cambridge Journal of Economics, 5, 1981

Cripps, Francis, 'Government Planning as a Means to Economic Recovery in the U.K., Cambridge Journal of Economics, 5, 1981

Crouch, Colin, 'The Essence of Politics', Socialist Commentary, September 1970

Davenport, Nicholas, The Split Society, London, Gollancz, 1964

Davies, G. and Piachaud, D., 'Why Public Spending has gone through the Roof', The Times, 8th July 1981

Drucker, H.M., Doctrine and Ethos in the Labour Party, London, Allen and Unwin, 1979

Field, Frank et al, To Him Who Hath, London, Penguin, 1977
(ed.), The Wealth Report, London, Routledge Kegan Paul, 1979

Fletcher, Raymond, 'Where did it all go wrong', Encounter, November 1969

Foot, Paul, The Politics of Harold Wilson, London, Penguin, 1968

Gamble, Andrew, 'The Free Economy and the Strong State', Socialist Register 1979

Glyn, Andrew, and Harrison, John, The British Economic Disaster, London, Pluto, 1980

Glyn, Andrew, and Sutcliffe, Bob, 'The Critical Condition of British Capital', New Left Review, 65, 1971

Gough, Ian, The Political Economy of the Welfare State, London, MacMillan, 1979

Hall, Peter, 'The Geography of the Kondratief Cycle', New Society, 26th March 1981

Harrod, Sir Roy, Towards a New Economic Policy, Manchester, Manchester University Press, 1967

Haseler, Stephen, The Gaitskellites: Revisionism in the British Labour Party 1951-64, London, MacMillan, 1969

Hatfield, Michael, The House the Left Built, London, Gollancz, 1978

Head, B.W., 'The Limits of Redistribution in the Capitalist Welfare State', A.P.S.A. Paper 1980

Howe, Brian, 'The Socialist Objective in the ALP', Seminar Paper Cunningham ALP

Howell, David, British Social Democracy, London, Croom Helm, 1976

Hughes, Barry, Exit Full Employment, Sydney, Angus and Robertson, 1980

Jenkins, Peter, 'The Labour Party and the Politics of Transition', Socialist Register 1977

Jessop, Bob, The State in Western Europe, London, Croom Helm, 1978

Johnson, David, 'Devaluation', New Left Review, 47, 1968

Kalecki, Michael, 'Political Aspects of Full Employment', Political Quarterly, 4, 1943

Keegan, Victor, ' Whatever Happened to the Creation of Wealth?', Guardian Weekly, 19th July 1981, p. 5
'The Spectre of Permanent Recession', Australian, 1st September 1981

Keynes, J.M., Essays in Persuasion, London, MacMillan, 1931
'National Self-Sufficiency', Yale Review, 22, 1933
The General Theory of Employment, Interest and Money, London MacMillan, 1973
Activities 1940-1946, London, MacMillan, 1980

Kidron, Michael, 'Labour's L-Shaped Alternative', New Statesman, 10th April 1981, p. 20

Kilpatrick, Andrew and Lawson, Tony, 'On the Nature of Industrial Decline in the U.K.', Cambridge Journal of Economics, 4, 1980

Kincaid, James, 'The Decline of the Welfare State', in Harris N. and Palmer J. (eds.), World Crisis, London, Hutchinson, 1971

Kogan, David, and Kogan, Maurice, The Battle for the Labour Party, London, Fontana, 1982

Lapping, Brian, The Labour Government 1964-70, London, Penguin, 1970

Leonard, Dick, 'Tribute to Crosland', The Economist, 19th February 1977, p. 15

Lipsey, David and Leonard, Dick (eds.), The Socialist Agenda: Crosland's Legacy, London, Cape 1981

London C.S.E. Group, 'Crisis, the Labour Movement and the Alternative Economic Strategy', Capital & Class, 8, 1979
The Alternative Economic Strategy, London, C.S.E., 1980

McDermott, Goffrey, Leader Lost: A biography of Hugh Gaitskell, London, Frewin, 1972.

Milliband, Ralph, 'Moving On', Socialist Register 1976
'The Future of Socialism in England', Socialist Register 1977

Overbeck, Henk, 'Finance Capital and the Crisis in Britain', Capital & Class, 11, 1980

Prior, Mike, 'Problems in Labour Politics: Interviews with Stuart Holland, Frank Field and Michael Meacher', Politics and Power 2, 1980

Purdy, David, 'The Left's Alternative Economic Strategy', Politics and Power 1, 1980

Przeworski, Adam, 'Social Democracy as a Historical Phenomenon', New Left Review, 122, 1980

Radice, Giles, 'Why the Labour Party must not Split', Guardian, 12th January 1981

Reglar, Steve, 'Keynes and his Critics', N. Wintrop (ed.), Democratic Theory and Its Critics, Flinders University/Croom Helm, 1982

Saville, John, 'Hugh Gaitskell: An Assessment', Socialist Register 1980

Scase, Richard, Social Democracy in Capitalist Society, London, Croom Helm, 1975
(ed.), The State in Western Europe, London, Croom Helm, 1978

Sked, Adam and Cook, Chris, Post War Britain: A Political History, London, Penguin, 1979

Skidelsky Robert, 'Keynes and the Reconstruction of Liberalism', Encounter, April 1979

Slee, Ron and Stokes, Geoff, 'Democratic Socialism', N. Wintrop (ed.), Democratic Theory and Its Critics, Flinders University/Croom Helm, 1982

Stewart, Margaret, Protest or Power, London, Allen and Unwin, 1974

Stewart, Michael, Labour and the Economy: A Socialist Strategy, London, Fabian Tract, 1972
The Jekyll and Hyde Years: Politics and Economic Policy Since 1964, London, Dent, 1977

Strachey, John, 'Tasks and Achievements of British Labour', New Fabian Essays, London, 1952

Sunday Times, 'The Day the Pound Nearly Died', Sunday Times 14/21/28 May 1978

Taylor, Graham, 'The Labour Government 1974-78', Marxism Today, October 1978

Thurow, Lester C., The Zero-Sum Society, New York, Basic Books, 1980

Tyrrel, R.E. Jnr. (ed.), The Future that Doesn't Work, New York, Doubleday, 1977

Vaizey, John, 'Disenchanted Left', Encounter, February 1968
'Anthony Crosland & Socialism', Encounter, August 1977

Westergaad, John, 'Social Policy and Class Inequalities', Socialist Register 1978

Williams, Phillip Maynard, Hugh Gaitskell, London, Cape, 1979

Whiteley, Paul, 'Who are the Labour Activists?', The Political Quarterly, 52, 2, 1981

Will, George F., 'Unpadding the "Padded Society"', Newsweek, 16th February 1981

Wolfe, Alan, 'Has Social Democracy a Future?', Comparative Politics, 11.1., 1978

Wyatt, Woodrow, What's Left of the Labour Party, London, Sidgwick & Jackson, 1977

Young, S. and Lowe, A.V., Intervention in the Mixed Economy, London, Croom Helm, 1974

INDEX

accountability (of Labour leadership and Labour MPs), 35, 36, 38, 40

Alternative Economic Strategy (AES), 19, 22, 23, 30, 36, 38, 49, 57

Atlee, Clement, 1, 4, 40

balance of payments, 6, 9-11, 18, 20, 26 27, 31, 33, 45, 48

Bank of England, 10, 30

bank rate; see interest rates

Barratt-Brown, Michael, 13, 15

Basnett, David, 35

Bayliss, William, 55

BBC Dimbleby lecture, 41

Benn, Tony, 18 19, 24 25, 26, 30, 32, 33, 34, 35, 36, 42, 43, 46, 47, 48, 49, 50, 53, 56, 57

Bevin, Ernest, 4

block vote, 40, 49

Brown, George, 12

bureaucratic centralism, 2, 41, 42, 45

business 'confidence', 3

by-elections, 22, 44, 51, 52, 53, 54, 56
Chester-le-Street 1973, 51; Lincoln 1973, 22; Warrington 1981, 44, 51; Croydon 1981, 52, 54; Crosby 1981, 54; Hillhead 1982, 53-4; Beaconsfield 1982, 55; Merton & Morden 1982, 55

Cambridge Economic Policy Group, 33, 43

Cambridge Econometrics, 44

Cambridge Journal of Economics, 47

Campaign for Democratic Socialism, 1

Callaghan government, 33, 34, 37

Callaghan, James, 1, 10, 11, 24, 30, 31, 32, 33, 35, 36, 38, 39

Castle, Barbara, 18

CBI (Confederation of British Industry), 26, 54

centre party, 38, 41

City of London, 11-12, 46

consensus politics, 7, 12, 47, 48

Conservative Party, 4, 26, 29, 33, 34, 35, 38, 40, 50, 51, 52, 53, 54, 56

constituency parties (Labour), 36, 39, 41, 56

corporatism, 34, 45, 46, 47

Council for Social Democracy, 40

Cripps, Francis, 47

Crosland, Anthony, 5, 6, 7, 8, 12, 13-5, 16, 17, 19, 22, 30, 31, 32, 42; and deflation, 12, 17, 31; and economic growth, 6, 12, 14, 17; and IMF intervention, 30-1; and mixed economy, 5, 7; and nationalisation, 6, 7, 8, 24 - of land, 24; and public expenditure, 14, 17, 31; and import controls, 30; and taxation, 14, 17

Croslandism, 40, 44

deflation (and orthodox deflationary programmes), 3, 10, 11-12, 18, 19, 20, 24, 26, 27, 30

demand management, 3, 27, 42, 48, 57

devaluation, 10, 11, 12, 20, 44, 45, 47
1967 devaluation, 10-11

education, 3, 7, 15, 25, 29, 45, 52

EEC (European Economic Community), 30, 31, 34, 37, 56
membership of, 22, 36, 39, 44, 56
referendum on, 22, 25, 26

EFTA, 10

electoral college, 39, 49

INDEX

INDEX